Poiesis
REVIEW

6

No. 6

Poiesis
REVIEW

· Various Authors ·

Alternating Current
Palo Alto, California

Poiesis Review No. 6
Various Authors
©2013 Alternating Current

Front cover artwork: "Deep Sea Garden." Back cover artwork: "Lost at Sea." Artwork by Terry Fan of Terry Fan Illustration, society6.com/artist/igo2cairo. Property of and ©2013 Terry Fan Illustration. Used with permission. All rights reserved.

Design and Editor: Leah Angstman
leahangstman.com

Technical Graphics Editor: Michael Litos

Alternating Current
Palo Alto, California

For the most current contact and ordering information, visit:
alternatingcurrentarts.com

ISBN-10: 0615927866
ISBN-13: 978-0615927862
First Edition: 2013

Nothing in life is to be feared; it is only to be understood. Now is the time to understand more, so that we may fear less.

—Marie Curie

Table of

CONTENTS

We Watch the Horse Fly Home

JANE STUART

Smiling sunlight dashes windowpanes
of foreign cars. The road is exquisite;
it stretches to eternity
and never winds outside a tunneled mound.

Streetlights, traffic accidents, the knot
of easy tourists with cameras hanging
on their arms
block the view a guidebook said
to look for.

But the response the horse makes,
keeping time beside gray buses,
anchors the unknown
and fills our life today with what was old.
When the moon shines and day sleeps,
we stay inside the wind that holds to night.

An unheard word, a honking,
flashing light, a dented bumper
finish what was modern; or was old.

The road is not to be remembered
and is there to be remembered
like a locket wrapped around
an alabaster neck. But the statue's wisdom
was foretold us—it is only memory
kept in two albums
that record this time.

No Sad Songs in the House of the Sun

SHAUNA OSBORN

I.

A father taught his five-year old
to memorize where they were
in relation to the air force base
no matter where they went:
the grocery store
church
school
her cousins' house.

He said it was important
in case anything bad happens:
bombs
explosions
coordinated air attacks—
& when it happened,
whatever it was,

> she had to run toward the base
> as fast as she could,
> tearing the clothes
> off her body
> if she saw a sky full of smoke.

> He said this would be a better,
> hopefully instant death,
> rather than the excruciating
> slow death that would happen
> if she were too far away.

II.

The daughter found pictures of explosions,
bombs, & air attacks
the next time they went to the library.

The books were thick,
so heavy the father had to help get them
from shelf to the table for her.
Books so old, so dusty,
housing lots of dark type
on bible-thin paper
with gray & black pictures
just like the old encyclopedias
her uncle had at home.

The destruction pictures
she found were funny—
like huge clouds
landed on the ground,
too tired & fat to float.

III.

A kindergarten teacher
had her class draw their families
for show & tell one day.
So the daughter drew herself, her sister,
& her dead brother—stick arms joined,
rushing toward the spot
their longer-legged parents
had just abandoned on the page.
All moving closer
to the crayoned iridescent gold,
burnt orange, & dandelion waves
coming from where the air base had once been—
waxy bright waves of doom
she thought were gorgeous,
like sunset hitting clean river water.

Blazon

PATRICK KINDIG

His apartment
was small. He stood
at the window
and everything smelled
of jasmine and salty
skin and his body
was cut by lines
of shadow conjured
by the slowly ripening
sun. His arms
were like arms and his golden hair
was like golden hair
and the slow curve of his hip
peeking through the slivering
gap between his T-shirt and
jeans was like the slow curve
of a hip. I watched him
prayerfully and the sun
lit the muscles of his back
with shadow and they were like
the muscles of a man's
back. He turned
toward me and the bridge
of his nose was straight like
the bridge of a nose. He was
still for a moment and stood
divided into precise pieces
of black and gold. Then
he stepped away from the window
and I thought of
Aschenbach's madness
and of everything
that has been said about
the beauty of bodies and he walked
toward me and he moved
like the lips of a river kissing
its way along the shore or

a bird swaying on the thin
branch of a willow tree or a hungry
mouth of fire swallowing
a field of wheat
dry and ready to be
consumed.

New Mexico farmhouse, hard to find after all those years

LEAH ANGSTMAN

A series of raps sounded at the farmhouse door, matching the heavy burden of the desert wind against bound shutters.

"Pinkerton, Mr. Westgate. I need you to come on and open up for me." The Pinkerton detective scanned his eyes across the dusty, dying ranch and back to the two men standing at either side of the closed door, guns drawn, still and silent as trained sentries. Nothing stirred, and the man realized he held his breath and galvanized himself for what he would do. *Westgate*—eh, he could rot in hell. The woman, however, would be innocent, but she'd be standing by the man she'd married, probably right that moment holding her own breath on the other side of the door.

The cranky drawl of rusted hinges split the heat, and the detective wiped his brow, allowing his gaze to sweep the lanky cowpoke glowering through the tiniest crack in the door. *Homemade door*, the Pinkerton corrected, *lopsided, sagging where the foundation had shifted, scraping a line of resistance into the floor at the rancher's spurs.* Westgate wore his spurs indoors: showed what kind of woman he'd married and eased the Pinkerton's

16

guilt—but not the twitchy finger that itched at the Union-issued Colt Navy that had outlived its glorier days.

An eyebrow cocked on Westgate's forehead. The years hadn't changed him. He was still an arrogant son of a bitch and held his set jaw like a murderer. A particularly cool snarl spoke for him: "Hell, Carson, it's been a while. Guess they don't pay you to leave jobs unfinished, huh?"

Detective Carson heard the click behind the door and could picture that LeMat Grapeshot, the way it had once glinted in the Texas sun as its barrel aimed at the base of a pretty girl's throat. Carson's wife had never let him wear his spurs in the house. *"Hang 'em up at the door,"* she'd always said, so sultry, so huskily. He'd always hung them up at the door, but no one asked him to, anymore.

In that second, one of the men standing guard scuffed a shoe, and a surprised Westgate moved swiftly to slam the door, lodging it instead upon Carson's much swifter boot. A string of oaths left both men's mouths, but Carson wedged his way inside, the Navy drawn, facing Westgate's LeMat. A woman shrieked and froze in the corner, and the two men narrowed eyes at each other, circling like feral cats.

"Make your move, Detective," Westgate hissed, spit flying from his mouth. "You've waited a long time for this."

"Yes, I have," Carson nearly whispered. "My God, yes, I have." Faster than an eye could blink, Carson drew his bead from Westgate and pulled the trigger, the detective's bullet whizzing through the air with a deafening pop and an accompanying whir. A heartbeat later, the woman slumped to the floor, a halo of red on the wall behind her, a hole clear through her throat.

Redhead

I have a girlfriend; she's 40 years older than I.
We say it's unfair to have met when age
and polio have left her youthfulness behind.
When I am with her, being is like breathing
and long silences are as productive as two-hour
conversations. Love often finds us this way—

Right person, wrong place
Wrong time, right person
Right woman, near death.

She told me that when I am 75,
I'll realize how everything only gets worse.
When the ones you love die, new ones no
longer take their place. But I tell her she's wrong.

Life dealt us its cruel card. We won't be jumping into
flaming beds with the passion of young bodies. Rather,
I will roll her wheelchair or lift her off the ground when
she topples over. I will be happy to hold her in my heart
as a perfect moment when love blew through the right
window at the wrong time.

CHARLES P. RIES

the dance

JUSTIN HYDE

let me
use your body
while your soul
is perverted
by opiates

let us
hurdle fog
scope and boundary
as we
approach blind drunkenness

let the
next day come
like a dragon
opening his eye

nothing left
but the
hundred-dollar
bar tab

and your smell
on my
hands.

Afternoons of Quatrains & Sonnets, Of Mandolins & Minotaurs ...

HOSHO McCREESH

And how refreshing:

finally giving
all this shit
up.

Surreptitious Spirit

Watching *Ghost Hunters* on TV; Jason and Grant,
simple plumbers during the day—
investigating ominous ghostly encounters,
elusive otherworldly entities, and restless
surreptitious spirits at night.
Reminds me of me,
a simple marketing communications manager
during the day—
a poet, a restless, surreptitious
Byronian spirit at night.

MICHAEL ESTABROOK

Featured Writer

NATHAN GRAZIANO

Nathan Graziano is a high school teacher with an MFA in fiction writing from The University of New Hampshire. He is the author of two collections of short prose, *Hangover Breakfasts* (Bottle of Smoke Press) and *Frostbite* (Green Bean Press); three collections of poetry, *Not So Profound* (GBP), *After the Honeymoon* (Sunnyoutside Press), and *Teaching Metaphors* (Sunnyoutside); and several chapbooks of fiction and poetry. His work has appeared in numerous literary publications, such as *Word Riot*, *The Hawaii Review*, *The Good Men Project*, *Night Train*, *Rattle*, and *Nerve Cowboy*. His short story, "Fishbone," was a finalist for The Norman Mailer Award in 2011, and he has a trophy to prove it. Nathan currently lives in Manchester, New Hampshire. Find him at nathangraziano.com.

Vandals

he first suggestion was toilet paper. Then, as I watched Geoff's gapped grin spread across his face, I knew that eggs were going to be involved, too.

Larry's house was going down.

It was Halloween in 1987, and I was twelve years old. The day before, my parents sat down my sister and me at the kitchen table to give us their speech—not to be confused with *The Speech*, the infinitely awkward birds and bees business. I never got that one from either of my parents. I learned about sex by flipping through a stack of *Hustler* magazines that Geoff's older brother, Paul, hid in his bedroom closet. After walking in and finding us with his magazines fanned out on the floor one day, Paul gave us the boiled-down-to-the-essentials version of *The Speech*. It went: "If your dick is pointing up, put a rubber on it."

Instead, my parents were about to give us the other speech no kid wants to hear. Mom sat across from Anna and me with her hands folded on the table, while my father paced back and forth behind her, his head down, puffing a Marlboro and palming a can of Budweiser.

Mom said, "We want you both to know that we love you very much, and this is in no way your fault." The muscles in her face tightened as she patted her eyes with a tissue she was holding.

I had been expecting this. The previous week, while my mom was working the second shift at the hospital,

NATHAN GRAZIANO

I overheard my father on the telephone in their bedroom, telling the person on the other line that he was leaving Mom. However, my sister Anna, who was two years younger than I, didn't suspect a thing. As soon as my mother told us they were getting a divorce, Anna leaped up from her chair and bolted to her room, her hands covering her face.

Then my parents started getting into it.

"That went well. Good plan, Julia," my father said, as he cracked open another can.

"Why do you always have to be such a son of a bitch, Don?"

"Our son is right here."

"He should know it, too. You're a son of a bitch."

I had enough and got up and went to Geoff's house. Geoff's mother, who divorced his dad when Geoff was too young to remember, worked two jobs and was hardly ever home. At first, Mom didn't want me going over there when his mother wasn't around, claiming she heard rumors about Geoff's older brother and didn't trust him to watch us. Now, with black pouches beneath her eyes and the skin on her face pale and drawn, Mom was tired of fighting—tired of fighting with me, tired of fighting with my father—and when I said I was going to Geoff's, she relented with a flick of her wrist.

My father didn't say a word. He didn't even look at me when I said I was leaving.

While Halloween was already ruined, for whatever reason, Geoff and I still felt the need to dress the trees in our neighbor's front yard with toilet paper and pelt his house with eggs.

By 3 p.m. on Halloween, we were sitting cross-legged on the floor in Geoff's bedroom, surrounded by the posters of our New England sports heroes. On one wall, Roger Clemens stood on the pitcher's mound, mid-delivery, his head turned to an imagined hitter. Beside it, Larry Bird was lining up a jumper on an invisible hoop, and across the room, on the closet door, Andre Tippett was about to level a crushing blow on some ghostly halfback trying to turn up the field. From the pillowcase he would later use to collect candy, Geoff pulled out two rolls of toilet paper and a carton with half a dozen eggs he lifted from his fridge.

"I have something else," he said, reaching under his bed for a shoebox filled with baseball cards, the entire 1986 Topps collection. He took something out of the shoebox and closed his hand around it. "Guess what it is."

"Your mother's underwear," I said, standing up. "Let's listen to Bon Jovi."

"Paul says Bon Jovi are homos. He says Jon Bon Jovi has AIDS, and we should listen to Metallica instead."

Shrugging, I rewound the cassette of *Slippery When Wet* in Geoff's deck to "Livin' on a Prayer." I liked the introduction, the voice box; and the couple in the song, staying together through all those hard times, reminded me of my parents—when they used to get along, that is. Like the guy in the song, my father once played the electric guitar in a band, and I remember when he sold his Stratocaster after his band broke up. That's when he started getting drunk *every* night.

"What's in your hand?" I said to Geoff.

Geoff held out his fist, unfurling one finger at a time. In his palm laid something that looked like a shriveled cigarette. "I stole it from my brother."

"What is it?"

"It's a joint, retard. It's supposed to make you go psycho," he said. "I figured we'd smoke it before hitting Larry's house tonight."

Panic shot down my arms, and my jaw hung open like it were attached by wires. As a pledged member of Nancy Reagan's *D.A.R.E.* program, I had signed a contract stating I'd "Just say no," and I'd seen the commercial with the fried egg—*this is your brain on drugs*—a million times. Drugs were bad, potentially deadly.

But there was another part of me that liked the idea of being bad and taking drugs. Little was I aware that this part of me would eventually seize control over my life, like it did with my father, and, eventually, this part of me would turn me into a son of a bitch, like my father, who was little help when it came to helping me make good decisions. On the night after

25

my fifth-grade teacher—a gray-haired woman who genuinely feared anything illegal—talked to us about marijuana, warning us that it could make you go crazy and fry your mind, I went home and asked my father if it were true, if smoking pot would make me go crazy. He grinned, shrugged, and opened a beer. "Ask your mother," he said. Soon after, Len Bias, the first-round draft pick for the Celtics, died from a cocaine overdose, and that was when Geoff, all the guys in our class, and I signed the *D.A.R.E.* pledge. Just say no. No way. Never.

Now. Maybe.

Someone knocked on the bedroom door, and Geoff's eyes widened. Terrified, he tossed the joint under his bed.

"Open the door, shit stain."

Geoff unlocked the door, and Paul strolled in, his thumbs hitched in the belt loops of his nut-hugger acid-washed jeans. He sported a faded Iron Maiden T-shirt and dirty-blond hair, feathered in the front and brushing his shoulders in the back. Immediately, he went to the cassette deck and shut off the music.

"Bon Jovi's a faggot," he said. "Listen, dildos, Deb's coming over, and I'm closing my door. If either of you interrupts us, I'll rip off your arms." He looked at me. "Does what's-her-name still babysit you?"

"Danielle," I said, although Paul knew her name and once shared a rather thorough list of things he would like to do, sexually, to her face. "She says you're a druggie."

"Tell her she's a slut," Paul said, running a black comb that surfaced from his back pocket through his hair. "She's got big tits, though. I'd like to suck on one of those melons, if you know what I mean."

I glanced at Geoff. While I had looked at the breasts on the girls in Paul's *Hustler* magazines, the appeal was not exactly sexual—yet. The thrill, instead, lay in seeing what I was clearly not meant to see, what was always being hidden from me. But that would soon change. Within two years, I'd be willing to crawl on my stomach through a pile of razor blades and shards of broken glass to get my hands on a set of breasts.

Paul then flipped us the double-birds, grabbed his balls, and made for the door. "Catch you later, faggots."

As soon as Paul left, Geoff was, again, holding the joint and letting it roll in his cupped hand. "This won't make us act like him, will it?"

My father didn't come home for dinner that night. This was the first time my father skipped dinner, the first of many dinners missed, until he would finally move out of the house and in with his girlfriend after New Year's.

Mom, still wearing her nurse's scrubs from work, tried to be nonchalant by humming "Bridge Over Troubled Water" while we waited. After twenty minutes with the pork chops and potatoes and green beans warming in the oven, she resigned herself to the fact that he wasn't coming home and told Anna and me to grab plates. Deep down, I think Mom still wanted their marriage to work, despite the fact that my father was cheating on her. For the first six months after he moved out, I would hear Mom on the phone at night with one of her sisters, her face to the kitchen wall, crying and spitting my father's name like it was poison. And it was.

My father, on the other hand, was already dating our babysitter's mother, Lynn, who would later become my stepmother, and he never mentioned Mom's name, unless Anna or I brought her up. Danielle stopped babysitting for us soon after my father stopped showing up for dinner.

At first, no one spoke at the kitchen table, and our silverware scraping the plates amplified the silence. Mom tried smiling, but her eyes, glossed-over and focused on the wall clock, weren't into it. Next, she tried awkward conversation.

"What are you going to dress as tonight, Vince?"

"I'm borrowing an Alf mask from Geoff," I said, without looking up from my plate.

"Are you going trick-or-treating, or are you too old for that?" While not oblivious to it, my mother found my approaching adolescence unsettling, bothersome, like a dull ache that's difficult to locate.

I continued to stare at my plate. "Maybe," I mumbled, careful to conceal my real plans.

I'm still not entirely sure why we were so hell bent on hitting Larry's house, or why we had to get high to do it. The ostensible reason, I guess, was that Larry—a beer-bellied man in his mid-thirties with a trimmed beard and narrow eyes—was an asshole. He was obsessed with his lawn and ornery about it, sometimes threatening the neighborhood kids who trespassed on it. While well aware of this, it still didn't stop me from cutting through his yard to get to Geoff's house. A couple of times, Larry caught me on his lawn and came to his door and screamed, threatening to call the cops as I sprinted away.

Larry and his wife were one of the few couples in our suburban neighborhood, which was twenty miles east of Providence, without kids of their own. And when it came to dealing with other people's children, Larry was a notorious dick, especially when it came to the boys. Rumors had circulated that Larry once pulled a shotgun on Mike Hague, whose family moved to Hawaii when I was in the second grade, but no one could prove the story. Paul and some of his stoner buddies swore it had happened, but no one actually saw it. Regardless, when Geoff and I were making plans to hit Larry's house that Halloween, that shotgun lingered in our minds like a phantom limb

"What about you, Anna?" Mom asked and smiled at my sister. But, again, Mom's eyes weren't into it. "Are you going out with your friends tonight?"

"You said you were going to take me out trick-or-treating."

"Did I?" My mom slapped her hand against her forehead. "That's right. I did." Her head jerked back like she'd been grabbed by the hair, then snapped forward into her hands. Then Mom—the unshakeable foundation in our family, the woman who made our meals and checked our homework and attended to our every need—was bawling into her small, thin hands.

Stunned and confused, I stood up and rubbed Mom's back as Anna draped her arms around Mom's neck. The weeping continued for what seemed a long time. In actuality, it was no longer than a minute.

Finally, Mom lifted her head and wiped her eyes with the backs of her hands. "That son of a bitch," she said, sniffling. Then she looked at me. "Don't grow up to be a son of a bitch."

"I won't."

And, lo and behold, I did.

Pell Elementary School was within walking distance of our houses, so when Geoff and I needed a spot to smoke the joint, we decided to go to the playground, which we knew would be dark and empty. We sat side by side on the swings with our feet dangling off the ground, trying to decide which end of the joint to light.

"My dad's cigarettes have filters," I said, the Alf mask—with its large latex snout and faux orange fur—on my lap. "Light the end with the filter."

"Joints don't have filters, you dumb shit." Geoff was dressed as a deranged hobo, wearing a faded pair of his father's old pants and red suspenders. With his mother's black eyeliner, he penciled a scruffy beard on his pale, freckled skin and was carrying a toy shotgun, which, he said, made him *deranged*. When he flicked the lighter, his bald face glowed in the flame and, for a moment, I could see what Geoff would look like as an adult. "I guess it doesn't matter which end I light," he said.

He placed the joint between his lips and slowly, like a lazy sunrise, lifted the flame to the end of it. The paper caught, and Geoff made a slurping noise like he was sucking through a straw. He held his breath as the smoke funneled from his nostrils and lips like an engine overheating, then he coughed a tremendous cloud, hacking for a good minute before handing me the joint.

"I can feel it already, Vince," he said. "I think I'm stoned."

"You're full of shit."

"I swear to God. I feel thick. Like my skin is really thick."

When I went to hit the joint, it had gone out, so I had to relight it and ended up torching half the thing in the process.

The paper burned unevenly, which I had never seen with my father's cigarettes, and I took a tiny hit, not giving the smoke the opportunity to fill my mouth before I was blowing it out and gagging. We went back and forth like this a couple of times, trying to seem casual and comfortable in our new roles as pot smokers.

But we weren't.

Then, a pair of headlights lit up the slide to the left of us. I was holding the joint and, horrified, dropped it on the ground and ran with Geoff into the woods beyond the playground. Hiding behind trees, we watched as a black Camaro parked in a teacher's spot outside the playground and switched off the headlights. With the engine running, the passenger door opened, and Whitesnake's "Here We Go Again" blasted from the car stereo. A girl got out.

"I'll be right back," the girl said and closed the car door. I recognized the voice as Danielle's, my babysitter, and although neither of us knew it at the time, in less than a year, she would become my stepsister.

The passenger window rolled down. "Do you want me to spark one?" called a male voice from inside the car. "You like to fuck when you're high, right?"

Danielle giggled. "I like to fuck when I'm not."

She approached the woods, humming something tuneless as her footsteps grew louder, like she was a character in a horror film, unaware of the madman who lurked in the darkness. Frozen by fear, Geoff and I held our breath. I put on my Alf mask, just in case.

A few feet into the woods, Danielle stopped and unbuckled her jeans, standing in front of the tree Geoff was hiding behind. From the corner of my eye, I watched as she pulled down her panties and squatted. Listening to her urinate thrilled me, much more than the naked women from the magazines. And by the time Danielle stood straight and zipped up, I had an erection that I didn't understand. I didn't feel high, just guilty.

As she was walking back to the car, Danielle stopped at the swings, bent down, and picked up the joint I dropped and sniffed it. "Hey Casey," she said, as she opened the car door, "you're never going to guess what I found."

Geoff looked at me and cocked his head in the direction of the woods. "Let's get out of here," he whispered, and we booked it back to the neighborhood with Larry's house lingering in our crosshairs.

"You don't feel anything? Not even lightheaded?"

"I don't feel anything," I said, taking off the Alf mask. The chilled night air felt good against my skin. The streets were mostly empty, and the porch lights were switched off. The October moon was almost full, with the exception of a nibble bitten off its corner, and the streetlights held our shadows, giant versions of us, on the concrete. I wanted to go home, but Geoff talked me into hitting Larry's house first. We decided not to toilet-paper the tree in front. It was too dangerous, and both of us were tired.

"I'm definitely feeling something," Geoff said, "but I'm not sure what it is. I think I'm high."

"I don't know," I said, conceding to a bit of lightheadedness. "Maybe I am, too."

We turned onto Larry's street, which had a cul-de-sac at the end and more woods beyond it. "What time do you have to be home?" Geoff asked.

I flipped on my mask. "My mom didn't say." And she hadn't. She had barely noticed me leave. "My parents are getting divorced," I said. It was the first time I said it aloud, and the words tumbled off my tongue like tiny stones.

"That sucks." Geoff held the pillowcase with the toilet paper and eggs in one hand and the toy shotgun in the other. "I don't remember my parents getting divorced. It seems like they've always hated each other." Then, Geoff grabbed me by the arm. "Stop. Get down."

We crouched behind a gray hatchback parked in front of Larry's house. The house lights were off, except for a window in the basement, where the bluish glow of a television set shimmered in the frame. Maybe Larry was watching a show with his wife, a thin woman named Fran. His wife usually worked the graveyard shift at the hospital, so people rarely saw her. The shade in one window, which I assume was their bedroom, was always pulled down during the daytime. Mom went to high school with Fran, and I remember Mom telling my father at dinner one night how she would occasionally run into Fran at the hospital. She told him that Fran and Larry were "still trying," which meant nothing to me at the time. If I'd understood it then, I like to think that I wouldn't have done what I was about to do. But that's probably not true. I was already beginning to show the signs of a son of a bitch.

Geoff reached in the pillowcase and handed me an egg. "After we throw them, run."

With the egg in the palm of my hand, I closed my fingers around it, and the egg seemed to disappear. My father would always brag about the wild things he did with his friends when he was younger. One time, he got arrested for getting drunk and streaking through the police station, and another time, one Halloween in high school, he and his buddies stole a bunch of pumpkins from people's front steps and put them on the principal's lawn. To the day he died of lung cancer, my dad liked to talk about playing with his band and going out to gigs and raising hell. Then, unfortunately, he had to grow up, or so he'd tell us, shaking his head while sipping a beer. He went and got married and had kids and nothing was ever fun again, he'd say. *Now*, I thought, *he's leaving us to have fun again.*

I wound up and threw the egg at the house. It hit the front siding beside the door. Geoff threw his and hit a window. The porch light switched on, and Geoff and I turned and sprinted down the street, running until we hit the woods, then stopping to catch our breath.

Geoff said, "That was awesome."

"Do you have any more eggs?"

"Four. Why?"

"Let's do it again."

"Do you feel high yet?"

"I'm definitely feeling something."

Born on Good Friday

NATHAN GRAZIANO

I skipped every mass on Ash Wednesday,
my forehead untouched, *sans* a priest's thumbprint.

I ate seven meatball subs during Holy Week,
when any good Catholic would've been fasting,

snuggling up with the hunger pains, half-constipated.
Instead, I held The Last Supper in my own kitchen.

Judas was drinking my beer and belching prayers;
Paul lost at solitaire, aching for a frozen corndog.

In the background, while watching the Red Sox game,
a commercial for *Catholics Come Home* aired on TV.

A clean-cut white guy, sober and fat, attested to how
reconnecting with Christ, like Jesus was his Facebook
     friend,

changed his life. Meanwhile, in a still-frame on the screen
beside him, there was a picture of a slovenly bearded man

with the same mouth—clearly his former heathen self
with bloodshot eyes and hair wild like weeds around a
     crucifix.

"There he is," I said to Peter, who was strictly a pothead,
"our thirteenth apostle, and he's bringing the roast beef."

But we all realized that thirteen was an unlucky number,
and Lent was never my thing, so we called for a pizza.

What My Doctor Said About My Mole

NATHAN GRAZIANO

I thought it was cancer, the malignant type,
my certain death. when a raised mole
on my left ass-cheek turned from brown to black.

I started to accept the idea of my early demise
and imagined my friends, drunk and devastated,
at my funeral, a mountain of soaked tissues
on a podium in the front of the funeral hall,
my casket behind them, as they all lied about what
a great guy I was, spinning fictions to make my
family forget the time I was lit at Thanksgiving
and announced my wife's first pregnancy
by shouting: "The old lady has a bun in the oven."

But that story won't be shared beside my coffin
where my cat will keep quiet vigil for days.

So I went to my doctor to have the mole checked,
and he told me it was a skin tag, something
people accumulate like ugly luggage
as they get older and their hides wither.

"Does it need to be removed?" I asked.

And my doctor said only if it bothered me.

Confessions of a Recovering Crier

NATHAN GRAZIANO

For three years, not one tear has streamed
down my cheek, not one wet lash to wish on.

As a younger man, with a thirst like baked dirt,
I would bawl over beers for hours, calling
friends at three a.m. during weeknight binges.

I'd sob into the phone: *I miss you, man,*
to my best friend, Dan, who was drunk in Missouri.

I fucked up my life, I'd cry to my wife,
while fixing, on ice, the evening's second nightcap.

One time in college, I fell from a stool
and puked on my shoes as the bar crowd applauded.
Then the bouncer slapped a stone-heavy hand
on my slumped shoulder and snarled, *Leave.*
I fell to my knees and pleaded and cried,
claiming I was framed by the bartender.

These days, I drink and cry less, and some people
have asked if I'm off the sauce. *No way,* I'll say,
but I'm a recovering crier. And I'll point to my eyes
as dry as hide and swell with what some call pride.

Opening Day

NATHAN GRAZIANO

he forecast is calling for rain on Opening Day—not showers, but a holy-shit-the-sky-is-pissing April downpour. He packs his books into the boxes he picked up at the liquor store, while his wife stands in the doorway to their bedroom, her arms crossed.

"Will you be out of the house by Thursday?" she says.

"It's Opening Day for the Red Sox," he says, and reaches onto the shelf for another handful of books, the McCarthy novels he read in a college course. "I'll be out by the weekend."

"Why doesn't your girlfriend help you move?" She says "girlfriend" like she's spitting poison from her mouth.

He rolls his eyes. "I don't have a girlfriend," he says. "She's a friend, and we were talking at a bar. She grabbed my cock, and I told her to quit it."

"I hate you."

"I know."

Calm and deliberate, he takes a box cutter from the pocket of his jeans. He'd like to slice a handful of her hair from her head, maybe scalp her a bit—nothing life threatening. Instead, he slices the duct tape and tosses another box of books into the corner of the room.

With her back again turned to him, his wife says, "Why can't you be out by Thursday? I can't stand seeing your lying ass around this house anymore."

"It's Opening Day"

"I just remembered that our son has baseball practice on Thursday," she says. "You said you'd bring him." Though he can't see it, his wife grins.

"It's supposed to rain," he says, and imagines the crack of a bat, the slap of ball hitting glove, the rustling of the stadium crowd, everyone waiting for nothing and everything. He imagines his son catching a pop fly and dying to tell him. He imagines the skinny kid staring into the stands and seeing only his mother's scowl, her bitter lips and slightly scalped head.

"I'll take him to practice," he says, and starts packing another box of books.

Sure, the girl grabbed his cock, but he wasn't surprised, and she wasn't his girlfriend. She's just some girl he invited to a ballgame, if it doesn't rain.

Beans

NATHAN GRAZIANO

hile splitting a pitcher with Toby—it was around noon last Tuesday—Toby started telling me how this girl he's been seeing calls pain pills "beans." He said this girl, who is half our age, crushes the beans into a powder, cooks the bean-powder on tin foil with a lighter, and then smokes the bean-rock from a glass pipe. Toby scores the beans for her from someone at the bar, but he won't tell me who it is.

"This girl—Erin—she can't legally order a drink. She's only twenty years old," Toby said to me, grinning. "I don't think you know her, Nick."

"I *do* know her," I said. "She used to work here as a waitress."

"Yeah, yeah," Toby said. "I forgot about that. She did work here."

Then, Toby told me that the other night, this girl Erin called him up, asking if he could score some beans. She told Toby, however, that she was broke that week because she had to pay rent to her grandparents. Toby said she lives with her grandparents in an old house around the corner from the high school, not far from the apartment where I now live with no one. Six months ago, I had a job and lived in a house with my wife and two kids. Now, I'm unemployed and live in an apartment with no one.

Toby told this girl Erin that he could score her beans, and she didn't need money, as long as she had a mouth—he winked at me. Toby then scored her the beans from some guy at the bar—I still don't know who it is—and this girl Erin went over to Toby's apartment to pick up the beans. Toby said as soon as she closed the door behind her, she dropped to her knees and started sucking him off.

I said, "I need to find a twenty-year-old girlfriend."

"That's not all," Toby said. "It gets better."

And here comes the weird part. From what Toby told me, all of a sudden, this girl Erin stopped sucking his cock and took a phone call. She stood up, held a finger to her lips, and then, walked into the other room. Toby said he zipped his pants, grabbed a brew from the fridge, and sat down to watch the basketball game. Ten minutes later, this girl Erin came stomping back into the living room, spiked her cell phone onto the couch, and kneeled in front of Toby.

Toby said he asked her what was wrong. "Her eyes and cheeks were streaked red, like war paint," he said.

So this girl Erin looks at Toby, rubbing her eyes, and said: "I just broke up with my boyfriend. The asshole called me 'a dumb bitch.' Talk about being disrespectful."

"Did you say *you* dumped *him* for being disrespectful to *you?*" Toby asked this girl Erin.

So, she told him the whole story. She said that earlier in the day, her boyfriend told her that he could smell cigarettes on her clothes, and this girl Erin had told him that she quit smoking. The boyfriend is really against doing any kind of drugs, so they started arguing about it on the phone, and he called her a "dumb bitch" for smoking again.

"But you smoke," Toby said to this girl Erin.

"I know," said this girl Erin, "but it was still a disrespectful thing to say to your girlfriend."

So, Toby asked her how long they had been dating, and the girl told Toby she had been dating this guy, Whatshisnuts, for two years. Then, Toby took a bean from his pocket and placed it gently in the palm of her hand, like it was a diamond ring.

"Only two years? I was married for almost ten," I said. "So?"

"So what," Toby said, as the waitress at the bar brought us another pitcher—it was my turn to buy. As I was handing the waitress a ten-spot, this girl Erin sent Toby a text message and wanted him to meet her someplace. Toby asked me if I wanted to meet this girl Erin and one of her friends at Applebee's at 3 p.m. and then go back to his place to drink beers and smoke beans with these twenty-year-old girls.

I looked at Toby, then at my beer, then at the white circle on my ring finger where I had worn my wedding band for a decade. I knew what I was going to do. Even though I still love my kids and my wife, I have hated myself lately. My hair is dusted gray, and I've gained weight, and I'm tired of sending out résumés.

Sometimes, we all need a bean.

For My Sister, on Her Wedding Day

NATHAN GRAZIANO

Take heed of the saints who sing among us.

Take heed of the saints who slow dance, ethereal,
among the delicate dust on the polished pews.

Take heed of The Saint who always said,
"Condemn the sin, but not the sinner."

Your strength, my sister, will always rest
in the easy way you smile, like a simple prayer,
while the house burns down around you.

Your strength, my sister, will always lie,
not in decibels of your yells or the way you play
a mythical fiddle but in the jokes you whisper
in your husband's ear, as the flames flick your faces.

Headlines

I'm obsessed with the news:
other people's tragedies
and thumbtack-sized triumphs,
the names without faces,
only ages and hometowns,
someone's life story in a blurb.

The Republicans have ruptured my stomach.
I've lost weight, and the neighbors think I'm sick.
My politics are falling off with my love handles.

I quit eating animal products
after an investigative report
that I watched on MSNBC
about the meat-packing industry.
In a former life, I now know,
I was an impotent stud.

NATHAN GRAZIANO

The Androgynous Coat

NATHAN GRAZIANO

I finished my beer, took a hit off the bowl Toby left packed on the coffee table, and grabbed my car keys. "Let's hit the bar," I called to Toby, who was in his bedroom.

"Come here for a second," he said.

Toby lived in a small second-floor apartment, not far from the room I rented after splitting with my wife. Devastated and still in love, I had resumed the behaviors I had stopped when I got married and had a family—bar-dwelling and barely eating and a wide variety of drugs Like a stumbling beast rising from the ashes of a calendar, in less than a month, I had become something unrecognizable to myself. Toby told me that he went through the same metamorphosis the year before, when he found out his now-ex-wife was sleeping with his cousin. Despite the fact that Toby—a former bodybuilder—was short and wide-shouldered, while I was the outline of an average middle-aged man, we now shared the same shadow.

When I walked into his bedroom, Toby had crushed up a Valium and cut it into two lines of fine blue powder on his dresser. He handed me a rolled dollar bill, and I went for it.

"Look at this coat," Toby said, and held up a red-and-black-checkered flannel jacket that, at first glance, appeared to be a hunting coat. "I picked it up at a yard sale," he said, taking the bill from my hand and snorting the second line. "What do you think?"

"You're asking the wrong guy. Fashion-wise, I never got over grunge."

"Look at this," he said, and put on the jacket and raised his arms. "Look at the pockets on this thing. There are pockets under the sleeves, by my ribs, and four pockets on the front."

"That's a lot of pockets."

"Fucking right, that's a lot of pockets. The other night, I put it on when Erin was here, and she told me it was a girl's coat."

"No shit," I said, and lit a cigarette—another bad habit I'd resumed. Erin, a twenty-year-old junky who had been sleeping with Toby in exchange for pain pills, had left a pair of silky black panties on Toby's bedroom floor. I picked them up and used them to clean my glasses. "She would know better than either of us."

"But why would they make a coat that fits me if it's for a girl? It doesn't make sense. What type of girl fits into this coat?"

"A big girl," I said. As the Valium massaged my temples with its feathery hands, I sat down on Toby's bed, closed my eyes, then fell back. My cell phone buzzed in the front pocket of my jeans, a million tiny pins vibrating down my leg. I grabbed the phone, saw a text message from my wife, and opened it: *ru @ the bar????*

"Fuck it, I'm wearing the coat to the bar," Toby said. "You ready to go?"

Melted into the mattress, I nodded my head. While in no condition to drive, I reached for my keys, not bothering to respond to my wife.

Toby and I took the two stools at the far end of the bar, beside a machine that played trivia if you fed it a buck. Toby kept the coat on, every now and then slipping his hand into a new pocket. As I drank more, my head began to nod, and I was almost asleep on my stool, when Toby punched me in the arm.

"Oh shit, Nick. This is not fucking good."

At the entrance to the bar, my wife stood with a man. The guy looked younger than we—my wife, Toby, and I were all forty years old—and he had a full head of black hair, compared to my thinning dome, washed gray. He wore a stylish black pea coat and a scarf. My wife, on the other hand, had on a blue-and-black-checkered flannel coat—Toby's coat, but a different color. My wife and I looked at each other. Her eyes were cold blue ice.

When I turned to Toby, he was taking off his coat. "I guess that answers that," he said.

I stared at my mug, wanting to hurl it across the bar at the head of the fuckwad in the pea coat. "It certainly does," I said, and reached for my beer.

Block Island, October 2011

The particle boards are slapped on the shop windows,
as the owners and employees and anyone-but-the-locals
wait for the five o'clock ferry, sipping Bloody Marys
at the Mohegan Bar, bags packed to head west for the
winter, to the Rockies, to ski resorts and seasonal work,
their incestuous ties to Colorado lift tickets and barstools.

We've come for the weekend, my wife and I,
dropping off our kids like laundry at my parents' house
and finding ourselves now on an empty beach, trolling
the coastline and scooping up slithers of sea glass.
I show Liz a smooth piece I found, red and translucent.
She lifts one hand to my cold cheek, scoops the slither
with the other; she thanks me and kisses my lips, quick.

I suggest we go back to the Mohegan Bar and order
a round of drinks, wait with the anyone-but-the-locals
for the five o'clock ferry—only so we can miss it.

NATHAN GRAZIANO

Hidden Bits of Glorious History

DAVID S. POINTER

The Commandant of the
Marine Corps had left his
garrison cover behind. I
suggested to my MP unit
that we call ahead to Supply
in Okinawa to have one
waiting for the general
upon touchdown, but
I'm outranked/overruled—
while a faster jet is fueled
and readied to transport
the military hat—now resting
on a red velvet pillow—
from Camp Pendleton
to Okinawa in lightning-strike
landing, as if it were
a rare artifact worthy of
great distances and
greater tax dollars.

Girlhood Games

PAULA CARY

Light as a feather,
Stiff as a board.
Light as a feather,
Stiff as a board.

Did you ever repeat
Such nonsense as I did?
Did you ever jump rope,
Chanting like I did?

I never taught you to fly
Over lava on the playground
Or how to dodge bullies,
Not that you ever had that problem.

All I know is
An entire generation
Passed between us,
And I know nothing,

Nothing of your
Girlhood games,
And you know nothing
Of mine.

Why I Have Mud on My Pants

HARRY CALHOUN

It's sleepytime for me, ten after twelve, doorbell rings twice,
at least half asleep I heard it twice, and I open the door
to rain beating down, and it's two policemen, and one
is a small white cotton puff and one is a bigger black cloud

and they don't know and I don't know
that they have the wrong address, but they've
woken me anyway, and they say, "We have a complaint,"
and I say, "Well, it's just me and my two black dogs,"

but only one peeks out from the kitchen,
and the black guy says, "Where's the other one?"
and I open the bedroom door, and sure as magic,
the shy female emerges. Then, the other cop says,

"Why do you have mud on your pants?"
And so I have to explain, still half asleep,
that when you let two Labradors out to pee
in a driving rain, you have a lot of mud to wipe off

their webby paws, and oh, by the way, you might want
to check on fifty-one-fifteen Lundy—a lot of people
mistake my house for that address, and they look at each other
and abruptly leave. Thanks for the visit and the grilling

and for waking me after midnight and especially thanks
for no apology. This is what I expect of my public servants.
And I lumber back to my bedroom to sleep, my two dogs in tow,
apparently still with mud on my sweatpants.

Say Goodbye

I give thanks for water
and the hope of birds.
I feel for the madwoman
I will never see again.

I want to take a last look
at the forest and the trees.
I say goodbye to the poet
and the woman I loved.

Everything is buried,
as I take my last breath.
I give my best to the shape
of clouds and the dead
in their resting places.

LUIS CUAUHTÉMOC BERRIOZÁBAL

Vervet Monkeys

K. M. DERSLEY

they eat the corn, and when
the men go after them, escape
into the bush; but when
the women give chase,
even if they wear trousers
and men's hats,
the monkeys see
or smell
through it all.

recently, they've started leering
and gesturing at the women's breasts
and crotches.
it seems as if they're getting ready
to launch sex assaults,
and of course then
they'll either have to be shot
or burned out.

my woman gathers well,
cooks good cassava,
and in the hammock,
she is pleasant.

let us praise bravery
for what bravery there is
in these women of ours,
oh, my brothers.

great of soul they are
and fearless,
because between the
cookfires and the stars
that burn on high,
between us
and the vervet gangs,
they walk the line.

Stp. Gran. Dad.

FRANKIE METRO

I had to wait
    for him to
call me a shithead
several times,
before I decided he
    looked like my grandfather,

the one who would
    come around on Sundays
and give me a fiver—
expressly for the collection plate
    at a Southern Baptist Church,
passed down a pew
that was shoddy
and put a crick in my neck
    that made me
blasphemous.

It's been a long time
    since Sunday school,
and I've desecrated
a few more
    altars since then ...

and even though I can hardly
    remember his first name anymore,
    I can still hear
that toothless, tobacco
stick whacking away
at our family tree,
    trying to shake out the
persimmons in my lungs—

a puckered fucker
    of a man
in John Deere coveralls
    and offensive breath.

It always smelled the worst
    when he would hand
me that fiver and say,
"It's for the plate,"
    to which I refused.

He would simply reply:
    "Shithead ... Shithead ... Shithead,"
and hold that crummy piece of paper
in the air
    until I finally took it.

God, Flying Makes Me Nervous

LAWRENCE GLADEVIEW

she said
grabbing my hand

looking out
the window
i slugged
the rest of
my whiskey
& hit the
attendant button

when the
stewardess
came by
i ordered
two drinks
& told
the lady
next to me
you need to loosen up

the attendant
brought us
our whiskeys
& when she asked
if there was
anything else
she could bring us
i told her
just keep 'em coming

as we
knocked back
our second glasses
i slowly slid
our
interlocked hands
in between
my legs
& thought to myself
damn
flying makes me
desperate.

Pea Soup

CHRISTINA ELAINE COLLINS

The moonbeam on the wall changes shape again: It's a swan's neck. No, a mermaid's tail. I wish it would make up its mind.

It doesn't matter because the beam is fading now. Dawn peeks through the parting in the curtains. He stirs in my periphery, yawning, stretching, turning toward me.

"Awake already?" He rubs his eyes.

I nod.

"Sleep well?"

"Not especially," I say.

"Was the room too cold?"

I shake my head.

"Too warm?"

I shake my head.

"Did I snore?"

I look at the ceiling. All night, it hid from me, but now I can see its vaults and patterns and painted angels, distractions that could have passed the time. It's amazing what daylight can do.

"I still feel the pea," I whisper. I don't know why I whisper.

He says nothing for a moment. He laughs. "But it's a different bed."

"She must have slipped another one under. I could feel it all night." I hear my words, their absurdity, but I cling to them.

He laughs again. "Why would she do that? You've already passed—"

"Find it funny, do you?"

"No. I mean—" He clears his throat. "Are you sure you didn't just roll over a button on your nightdress?"

"I'm sure."

"All right. All right. Let's have a look." He yawns and rolls out of bed. He lifts the mattress and peers under it dramatically, as if indulging a child. "I don't see anything."

I lift from the other side and squint into the shadows. "Of course not. It's too dark."

"Not much I can do about that."

I drop the mattress. "Your mother is conspiring to make me miserable. And you don't care."

He looks at me, blinking. I look back, not blinking.

"Fine," he says. "I'll get the servants to check. All right?"

The servants come, and I watch them pull off the sheets, shake them out, lift the mattress, flip it, examine every inch.

One of them shrugs. "No pea."

I shake my head. "She must have put it *in* the mattress. Tear it open."

They stare at me. They glance at each other, not sure whether to laugh or to stay silent. They look to my husband for guidance. He shrugs, too.

A vein in my eyelid twitches. I stand firmly under their stares, but sweat coats my underarms. I look at the bare bed. There is no pea, of course. Only the pea-sized ache above my left eyebrow.

It was wishful thinking.

After a minute, I wave them away.

I dress and wander down the hall. I'll be late for breakfast; I keep wandering. I enter the museum wing. It is already filled with visitors, throngs of people so absorbed in the exhibits that I don't worry about being recognized. Portraits of deceased rulers and ancestors line the walls. Display cases show off old trinkets and heirlooms that no one cares about. I walk past them, following the people. They crowd around a new exhibit.

The green vegetable shines in the case, polished to perfection. It's impressively round for having sat under twenty mattresses; the curator must have reshaped it. The plaque reads: *This pea was used in a test designed to identify the most sensitive, compassionate suitor for His Highness Harald Norway. The successful candidate, Her Highness Hannah Denmark, felt this pea through twenty mattresses; only a woman with a truly delicate sense of feeling could have done so.*

Harald's mother must have chosen the wording. I've never seen anyone so happy to hear I had a horrible night's sleep.

I'm impressed by how fast they put the pea on display. We were only married yesterday, and I only slept on the pea the night before that.

I'd hate to tell them and ruin their story. I'd hate to tell them that the pea had nothing to do with it.

I miss the pea. At least then I had an explanation.

Swirling spots. Vein-like shapes. Deep red shadows. These are the things I see on the backs of my eyelids. These are the things most people don't see, because they are asleep.

It's hard to explain the unsleep. We are not unlike the undead: bodies drifting about in the sunlight, seeming alive, awake, but not. I say *we* because I assume there are others. Somewhere. I can't be the only one.

I used to be like the rest: I used to sleep. I wish I could remember what it was like. I only remember waking. And running. Yes, I remember running when I was small, young enough to play outside. Running and swimming and horseback riding all day, until I was so exhausted that, by bedtime, I couldn't keep my eyes open.

I can't remember when I stopped running, when the world needed me to sit down more, at tables, at tournaments, at sewing lessons, at tea, all day. But that must have been when I crossed over, to the unsleep.

All I know now are these spots, shapes, and shadows. When I am bored of them, I open my eyes and stare at the moonbeam on the wall, watching it play its usual tricks. It's a mermaid's tail. No, a swan's neck. I can't decide.

I close my eyes again, but my lids sting. The unsleep is like that. It plays opposites. You try to be still, to relax your body, but then, you feel an itch on your leg. You scratch it. Then, your ear. You scratch it. Then, your forehead. Your cheek, your arm, your stomach, places you didn't even know could itch. You notice the taunt of the grandfather clock. *Ticka. Ticka. Ticka.* You wonder how long you've been lying there. An hour? Three hours? More? You don't want to get up because that will only delay things, put more distance between you and sleep, wasting the little time left before you have to go to breakfast. All you can do is wait and watch the moonbeam on the wall.

I recall stories I've heard, of a maiden somewhere in France or Italy, who is cursed to sleep a hundred years. Curse? I laugh in the dark. If that's a curse, I wish someone would put a curse on me.

I thought it might go away if I left, moved, removed myself from the stillness of home. Maybe I could sleep in other places. I'd never tried. Maybe that's why I didn't hesitate when my father took my hand in his bony one and gave me a reason to leave. What else do you do, when someone you love is dying before you? You promise to do whatever he wants— you'll marry the one he names; you'll form the alliance his people have long needed. You say yes. You agree to his final request, as he parts from this world.

But I did it out of selfishness as much as obligation.

Of course, it had been storming when I set out; that set the wrong tone. By the time I arrived, I was so wet and frigid that I didn't care. I just wanted to sleep. When I saw the twenty mattresses, I didn't see a test. I saw some odd sleeping custom, probably, of this new land, and mostly, I saw extra back support. I was willing to try anything.

The moonbeam fades, and the sun rises again. It sneaks up every time, though it takes a lifetime to get here. The household will wake soon, and I will rise, to float through the day.

Float through breakfast. Float through church. Float through tea. Float through this meeting and that tournament. Float through needlework and prayers.

Float through dinner.

I gather the green bits into a far corner of my plate. A dozen dainty beads, petite spheres, rolling around. I press my fork down, and the spheres collapse. The green insides ooze out, soft, squishy, delicate.

I suppose she thought it would be funny. Peas for dinner.

My mother-in-law works her fork like a frog's tongue, snatching up her peas and bringing them to her mouth in sharp, quick motions. "Ficky, are we?" She grins across the table. "It's all right. That's why we chose you."

"I'm allergic," I lie.

"Shame. Peas are my favorite food."

"I can tell."

"You don't have to eat them, if you don't like them. No need to pretend about allergies." She smiles at her son. "Right, Harald? No pretense here."

"Right." He smiles back, but the smile fades when he glances at me. I wonder if he suspects. Maybe I woke him last night with my shifting. Side to back to stomach to side. I tried to stay still for more than two minutes; I did. But it's hard.

Maybe he didn't notice.

I yawn.

His mother sees. Her smile fades, too. "You look tired." She says it the same way every time. No concern in her voice—just annoyance.

The only response I can think of is *Thank you*, so I say nothing.

Harald excuses himself to use the washroom. I hate him for leaving me alone with her.

She chews her peas and watches me. After a few mouthfuls, she chuckles. "Sorry about that test, by the way. Hope you didn't feel deceived. I just want the best for him, you know. He's all I have. It was nothing against you."

I blink. "Of course."

She smiles. "More pea?"

"Pardon?"

She blinks and gestures to the teapot. "More tea?"

I could have sworn she said ... I shake my head. "No, thank you."

She resumes eating her peas. I press my fork down and crush the rest of mine.

As I float through the days, I see, taste, feel, smell, hear, behind a veil. I exist this way, my senses at half-mast. The unsleep are used to half-living. As I walk past the parlor, I half-hear the voices.

"This isn't what I had in mind."

"I know, Mum."

I pause outside the doorway. Mother and son, having their daily chat.

"She has no energy. She's always yawning. Never adds to the conversation."

"What do you want me to do?" I strain to hear Harald; he speaks quietly, unlike his mother.

"And those dark circles under her eyes—they aren't becoming."

"Maybe your test overlooked something."

"What do you mean? My test is a perfectly accurate measure of sensi—"

"That's just it, Mum. It's not that she's sensitive. She's an insomniac."

Silence.

A sigh.

More silence.

I hear her clear her throat. "Well, we can't tell anyone. Not after the big to-do we made about the pea."

"No. Suppose not."

"And we'd lose the tourists, the extra commerce."

"True. Can't take it back now."

"We'll just get her some of those pills. The ones they use at the sleep clinics."

"Yes. That should help."

I turn away.

I walk down the hall toward the museum wing. I like to go at this time, evening, after the museum has closed to the public; it's quiet.

The pea sleeps peacefully in its display case. The glass is frosty; it becomes a freezer after hours. The pea can live forever this way.

I hold my thumb and pointer finger up to the glass, sizing the pea between them. I move my fingers to the ache above my left eyebrow. It's the same size: so small that I ought to be able to scoop it out of my forehead with a spoon or cut it out with a knife.

I eye the broom resting against the display case; a maid must have left it.

I half-feel myself pick it up, raise it over my shoulder, and bring it down on the glass.

The shards scatter around the pea and across the floor. I pick up the pea between my fingers. I could pinch it, squash it, mash it, right here, right now. Chuck it at the floor. Stomp on it, until it's nothing but a streak of guts. But would that be its most fitting fate?

I hear footsteps, shouting. Guards, probably, racing toward the pea room, stirred by the sound of shattering glass. I close my hand over the pea and flee.

I am the first to reach the dining room, cupping the pea in my palm, wiping blood off on my dress. Convenient that I wore red today.

I move toward the table. It's six o'clock, and the table is set with three bowls, covered to keep in the heat. I lift a lid and peer into the bowl. Steaming broth with floating green bits. Pea soup. Of course.

I drop the pea into the bowl at my left, not sure who will sit there tonight. They like to alternate.

I take my seat and wait. They enter two minutes later. Harald takes the seat at my right, and his mother sits at my left. She picks up her spoon. They start to talk about politics and peasant laws. I pretend to sip my soup while I watch her eat, spoonful by spoonful. I imagine the pea sliding down her throat, quietly, daintily. She cleans her bowl.

The door swings open. A guard bursts in, red in the face. "The pea," he pants, "has been stolen."

Harald pushes back his chair. My mother-in-law drops her spoon. She stands, clutching her stomach and looking green.

"Who took it?" she croaks.

The guard wipes his forehead. "No one saw. It must have been someone who lives in the palace—someone with easy access."

Harald narrows his eyes on his mother. "Did you anger anyone recently?"

She huffs. "Me? No. Unless you count a few mutterings here and there."

"What *kind* of mutterings?"

She shrugs. "Nothing harsh. I may have threatened to fire the constable. But I do that all the time. And I may have said something to the cook, about his choice of seasoning, but I hardly think that would—"

"The cook?" The guard's eyes widen.

My mother-in-law frowns back, then turns greener. She looks at her son. He looks back. Their gaze slides to the soup.

They all pounce on the table at once. I watch them spoon through the remaining broth: three poor fools searching for something they'll never find.

In their distraction, I slip away. I hurry through the halls, through a door, and another door. No one tries to stop me. All the guards must be looking for the pea. I push through another door and another, until there are no more doors, and I am outside, running.

I keep running.

Running, like I did when I was small.

I am running forever, I think.

The countryside stretches, emerald and gold and red and other colors I used to know. The hill slopes down for another mile or two, until the dusk rises and, with it, a farm. Cows graze in the field; I wonder if this is where my morning milk comes from. I squint at the farmhouse, tilted but round in places, like an old shoe. The hanging sign is tilted, too: *Vacancy*. I slow, my legs numb. My muscles ache from head to foot. I walk up to the door and push it open. A woman at the front desk looks up.

"I'd like a room, please."

She eyes my gown, muddied and sweat-soaked. "'Course, but I'm afraid we haven't got anything too fine."

"Doesn't matter. I just want a place to sleep."

She nods. "You look tired."

I recall all the times I've heard those words from Harald's mother. I blink. The way this woman says it, though—there's no condescension in her voice. No disapproval. Just understanding.

She takes a key off a hook on the wall. "I've got one open room. This way." I follow her up the stairs.

The room is small and empty but for a dresser, a washbasin, and a cot. The window is open. The woman leaves me, and I walk over to the window and watch children play in the fields. There are nearly a dozen of them. They must be her children, the woman's; they have the same red hair. Their laughter trickles up to me. I catch the scent of grass, and something else. I sniff, struggling to place it.

Fresh air.

I leave the window open and drop onto the cot. The mattress is thin and lumpy and sags in the middle. I lie on my back, close my eyes, and sleep like a rock. No—like a pea.

The Postcard

(after reading Paul Bowles'
The Sheltering Sky)

WILLIAM TAYLOR, JR.

At some point you realize
you've been gone too far
for too long
and you understand
there's no way back

and you write this on a postcard
and you give it to a man
but cannot tell him
where you want it
to be sent.

you hear the tiny clickings
of all the doors
as they close behind you

one by one

and there's a moment of honest sorrow
for everything lost

and then there is nothing
behind or in front of you

just the enormous sky
and the endless desert

and you turn to face it
embracing the terrible mercy
of forgetting.

Hemidemisemisphere —West

CEE

Hate
Hate of Hate
Restraint of hate through Hate
Destruction of all Hate
Hatefully
With foot massages

Teeter–

Totter—those marvelous constructions of
childhood, cemented into every
urban playground.

Are they designed to teach us balance,
as in Scales of Justice?

Or equality, as in even-steven?

More likely stability, as in: you can stay afloat
only if my sack weighs as much as yours—

only if my good days are longer than
my bad days.

How to live like this, how to recognize
one endorphin from another—

How to set priorities, be discriminating,
not be labeled a dilettante.

~

What do I do if you decide God may exist,
after all? As Creator, a Progenitor, a Judge?

I love you; I lean on your intelligence.
I juggle words and worth through your perceptions.
I would have to consider the possibility,

and I would tremble.

ANGELA CONSOLO MANKIEWICZ

3 in the Mourning

JASON FISK

He sat on the floor
in the purple music room
The lights were adjusted
just so
He sat down
crossed his legs
and leaned back
against the wall
He listened to record
after record
after record
There was a dirty spot
on the purple wall
where his head rested
He knew he needed food
but feared going out
into the world
The last time he left
he thought he heard
the Earth scrape
something
as it orbited the sun
and he looked to see
if others had noticed
and was scared
because they hadn't

He looked at the clock
and was relieved it was 3 a.m.
Nothing would be open now

He'd check the clock again later
There was time

Kleshas

We are human
because we love,
because life is more
than come-from-behind
grunting and reproduction.

We find truths
painful and necessary,
even if they leave us
bleeding quietly
on the roadside.

This form, humanity, we can't escape
with our patterns often animal—
feral and fighting against the upper syntax
in our brains to find this life simple and rote.

In the end, we succumb to nature's dealings;
we swallow the birth given to us
and understand hiding is never an option.

ALEATHIA DREHMER

We'll Ride

KEVIN M. HIBSHMAN

We'll ride again through counties wide
And open like a friendly hand.
We'll see things we need to see again,
Breathe free as reverent only we bend.
We'll ride.
We'll ride upon the plains, my friend.
Pathways once thought abandoned
Shall accommodate our passing.
Fragrant fields forlorn and asking to be kissed
By a lover's eye.
For those who passed this way before
Have recourse to a luck unchanging.
Time and tide do strive to deride us, but memory
Shimmers brighter in a light that does not blind us.
Here in this wild, as wraiths shall we glimmer!
No footprints leaving, but a gentle attar
Each spring to return.
We flower, and for a time appear spent.
Shedding leaves upon the matted grounds of fall.
Aged like wine, our laughter ferments
And echoes from every canyon wall.

"A black day in a black month in a black year in a black life with time to kill"

(—David Peace)

ALAN CATLIN

in twenty-dollar-an-hour
lost-love motels—mirrors on
the ceilings extra, magic-fingers
mattresses, one-armed coin-operated
bandits, black lights and red-tasseled
lampshades, scream-proofed walls,
leather bonds and shackles for your chains,
whips available, as well, ask at the desk—
the twenty-four-hour-a-day night clerks
possess all the keys to all the doors,
closets—always a pleasure to serve,
cash-only discounts for consenting adults,
the Mann Act no longer applies here—
this close to hell's open hearth, everything
is permitted—calls for the dead rerouted
overseas, where all the women are waiting
to be held in your arms.

The Efficacy
of Poetry

MERILYN JACKSON

What the fuck's it for—
poetry—anyway?
It doesn't give back what was yours.
It doesn't pick you up from all fours.

When we need it most:
Funerals, the end of love affairs,
the birth of a child,
the cresting of delphiniums,
the blistering of desert heat,
the dark of night, dawn—
does it slake our thirst,
deaden pain,
mollify our fear of the unspeakable
breathing of cheeses?
(Not to speak of crying your tears.)

Or *these* tears, cracking laughter,
ringaringaroses,
triangles of reference,
The Finger of God,
chitchat on that porch,
and that halleluwhat?

What is poetry for?
Does it give us closure?
What a concept. What a conceit.
Who came up with that?
I'd like to stick his hand down
my garbage disposal
before he writes his next.

The only closure is death.
And everything between birth and death
—poetry.

Die Vögel

(*The Birds*)

Mark ran ahead to the statue in the middle of the square. Thomas quickened his pace to catch up, but he did not run. It had rained that morning, and the few people Thomas saw in the square were clearly only passing through. Beyond the square, he could see the pale blue domes of the Berlin Cathedral. They looked like robin's eggs against the gray sky.

Thomas reached the statue. Mark was trying to climb into the lap of a sitting Karl Marx, but the statue was slick with rain from that morning, and Mark could not settle himself. Thomas leaned against Friedrich Engels' open hand and watched Mark slide around. Mark's jeans were soaked.

"Come on!" Mark said. "Climb up his arm!"

"*Nee, danke*," Thomas replied. He smiled as Mark slipped and grabbed at Karl's beard for support.

"Ach!" Mark steadied himself for a moment. "At least make a photo of me, then."

Thomas backed up and pulled out his camera. He made sure to get the cathedral in the background of the shot. When Thomas had taken the picture, Mark let himself tumble to the ground, landing on his feet.

"*Jetzt bist du dran*[1]," Mark said, taking the camera and pulling Thomas toward the statue by his wrist. "Don't worry about getting wet. I dried it all for you with my ass."

Thomas climbed up the statue awkwardly and held himself there. A woman walked by holding the hands of two

---

[1] *Now, it's your turn.*

quiet little boys and looked at him as if he had snuck into her backyard. He smiled sheepishly. Mark took the picture and Thomas jumped down clumsily, twisting his ankle.

"*Schon gut?*[2]" Mark asked. He looked at Thomas' ankle with concern.

"*Ja.* Could we take a break from walking, though?"

"Of course. I'll get food, and we can eat lunch."

"*Wunderbar.*"

Thomas limped a little, as they left the square and found a bench on a bridge. It was wet, but Thomas sat down anyway. Mark made Thomas lift his injured leg onto the bench so that Mark could look at the twisted ankle. It was already beginning to feel better, but Mark wanted to make sure it was not sprained or broken. He lightly pressed on Thomas' bones with the pads of his fingers, until Mark was convinced it was not a serious injury. Then, he went to get food.

Thomas watched him until he reached the end of the bridge and turned the corner. Thomas then turned and looked out over the Spree. The sky was growing darker and the wind was picking up. It looked like it was going to rain again. Very few people crossed in front of him on the bridge.

He liked feeling like he knew no one in the city. He also liked thinking in a language that was private here. He could disappear in the heart of Berlin, and no one would care enough to be angry with him for being careless. This thought was very comforting.

But Thomas knew that this was not actually the case. Mark would notice if Thomas disappeared.

He was not sure how he felt about this. He was not sure how he felt about Mark. Being with him was like being alone, but in German. Most of Thomas' memories were in English, and he liked how fuzzy they got when he was with Mark. Thomas spoke mostly German and Mark spoke mostly English when they were together. Neither of them spoke enough of the other's language to communicate well. They mostly did things with or next to each other.

Thomas did not know much about Mark. He knew that Mark enjoyed open spaces, like parks and squares, and that his chin was always rough with stubble no matter how

---

[2] *All right?*

recently he had shaved, but Thomas did not know what Mark thought of the world. Thomas liked not knowing this. It allowed him to imagine that all of the words Mark could not say in English were profundities in German.

A duck flapped its wings on the river below, then disappeared under the bridge. Thomas watched it go and smiled. It began to rain a little. Thomas was very happy here. He hoped that this happiness would not disappear when he left in a few days, but he knew it would, and this made him even happier. He looked down to the end of the bridge to see if Mark had returned yet, but he had not. Knowing that Mark was not back quite yet, but that he would be back soon, also made Thomas happy.

A young couple walked by pushing a stroller. The woman looked tired and cold, and the man looked worried. Thomas could not see the baby in the stroller. He watched the family pass in front of him. He thought that it must be warm and cozy in the stroller, and he was happy for the baby. Then, the woman leaned her head against the man's shoulder, and the man kissed the top of her head, and Thomas' happiness fell apart. He felt like he had been riding a bicycle uphill and had been near the top, but then, the gears on his bicycle had slipped past one another, and he was falling backward. He turned his head away and looked down into the river.

He had had a similar feeling before. The summer after he graduated high school, he met a girl at the coffee shop where he worked. She had been his first real girlfriend. She told him that she loved him, and he lost his virginity to her one night in late August, after he convinced himself that he loved her, too. Afterward, they had lain on the couch in her student apartment for a long time, saying nothing. Thomas had looked out the window at the moon and felt that he had achieved everything he ever wanted. Then, he stopped looking at the moon and looked at her face. Her eyes were closed. She did not exactly smile, but Thomas saw in her face the type of trust that small children have in their parents, and he knew that she was happy and certain. It was then that his own happiness had broken, and he had felt shamefully empty.

He felt almost like this, now. The passing family made him feel like an eggshell with the yoke blown out of it.

He thought of how he was a ghost in Berlin and of how he had to fly home soon; then, he thought of Mark. Thomas knew that Mark was not someone he could be with forever. That was all right. But he also knew that he could never really go home, now that he had met Mark. He thought of the time, when he was very young, that he had seen a baby bird fall out of its nest. He had picked it up and put it back in the nest, but his father told him that its mother would push the baby back out because it smelled like human now—that it would probably starve to death. At the time, Thomas had not understood how helping the chick back to its nest was wrong. Now, he thought he could understand things from the chick's perspective.

The duck that had disappeared under the bridge a while ago reappeared, now with another duck. They swam in circles below Thomas, and he watched them, until his eyes got lost in the swirling of the water.

"I hope you like Döner," Mark said. He had crossed the bridge without Thomas noticing.

"I love Döner," Thomas replied, looking up at Mark and smiling.

Mark was holding two Döner in one hand and two beers in the other. They always drank beer when they were together.

"Fantastic," Mark said. He smiled back and handed Thomas a Döner and a beer.

"*Danke schön,*" Thomas said, slipping into German. The rain had stopped, but Thomas knew it would start again soon. He opened his beer and took a bite of his sandwich. It tasted salty and spicy, and he savored its strangeness. He knew he would not be able to buy Döner when he was back in the States. He took a sip of beer and ate the rest of his sandwich hungrily.

Jet-Age Neuromuscular Junction

DAVID S. POINTER

when suicide rates trend upward
   like crumbling steps
when graffiti artists can't paint
   over the galvanized black
when spy cameras come
   and extreme-weather sirens do not
when computer interface problems
   are financial elite solutions
when innovative war tactics
   are more important than incubator babies
when humanity admits chopping down
   black cherry birch trees
when the periodic tables of human possibility
   float on higher
ground like the dogface butterfly
   onto red monkey flowers

Pact

I bought into
the system
of the Beast
believing
that I was an innocent
priest of a religion
culture   and art
but I was betrayed
by the Beast who always
wanted only to swallow
souls
and I betrayed myself
to survive   to join
the bourgeoisie
the middle class
being mediocre
holding mediocre standards
what will pass
mediocre dreams
pleasure   ease
as much luxury
and self-importance
as can be
patched together

ROBERT SCHULER

Still Victory

evidence of her tears
glistened her cheekbones
unlike morning's dew
reflecting the rising sun's
birth
instead, a slimy trail left by a dying worm
coating an afternoon's sun-seared asphalt
two junkies
and there, our son
newly ushered into a world he never inhaled
tiny fists ready to go, though already forever defeated
the little bastard's expression
mirrored, summed up, captured
my life
on his clenched-up, dead, sourpuss face
twisted with disappointment
our lone bond
that's my boy
that's my
boy

DENIS SHEEHAN

Requiem

My mother used to try to
hook me up with her boyfriends
while my father was at the store.
She'd tell her men how pretty
I was, how talented,
how smart. Then, she'd tell me
how [whomever it was this week]
& I had so much in common.
Dad would silently clock
the conversation,
thumb slowly through
the Sunday paper, &
glance up every few
seconds. Sometimes, the
guys would take Mom's
lead, ask me questions,
put their arms around
my shoulders, stare
at my breasts.

I always felt dirty—
stained by something
soap couldn't wash off.
By the time I was sixteen,
I'd move backward if
they came too close,
wore baggy clothes, &
never washed my hair.

SHAUNA OSBORN

Dad had quit marking
the show, but still refused
to let me stay home.
He never stayed near
the cash register,
going straight back to
the cooler to stock
cases of beer & soda.
When I went back
to help him, hoping to go
home soon, he'd hide the
open beer bottles
behind stacks of the
plastic bottle cases
& tell me to go
get more Dr. Pepper.

Bitter pills don't dissolve past six feet down

LEAH ANGSTMAN

I stood over him, compelled still to
argue our last bitter words.
"I cried harder when Paul Newman died,"
the only thing willfully dragged from my lips.

Guilt will eat at you
through time's unforgiving demands:
a grave thousands of miles away now, I yearn
to stand over it and admit
the last things we say
are not the first things we mean.

There is no life after death.
We go to the ground with the final words spoken
being the final words heard.
He does not somehow miraculously know
our bitter end
was false in everything
except its end.

The finality of anger lingers
until it has no reason to—
the only things truly final:
the things we left behind,
buried in the ground,
resurfacing in our wake;
the pills we thought we'd swallowed;
the names sworn eternally unspoken;
the forgotten
still remembered
with conscience-stricken fixation
toward its finality.

The only thing miraculous here:
how long, through miles and years,
guilt can truly last.

violence or violins

ANGIE TURNER JEFFREYS

The orchestra consisted of three instruments and three

instruments only piano cello and violence in retrospect these

last instruments may have simply been violins

perhaps I'd misheard
my father when he explained this minute

detail though would prove to be nearly Chaos

for the young girl

who grew up she's me twinkling the

dream that *violence* could hurt no more than string melodies

bumping bridges and wood inside my ears

then wars launched red sprays

I called them the symphonies that look just like I bet Jackson Pollock's inner pain could

had he but a country and buckets of brushes to ink

not blue colors in the skies

My Sister's Miscarriage

JASON FISK

I stood there as they squirted
the jelly on my sister's belly
and was reminded of how my wife
giggled every time that had been done to her.
I stood there and sobbed silently
behind my sister as I saw
the baby on the screen—
but saw no movement.
I was used to hearing
the speedy little machine-gun
heartbeat of my children,
but immediately knew something
was wrong; the baby
just floated there in her womb.

The doctor walked us through
the ghostly images on the screen—
This is the baby's head ...
Here's the ribcage ...
This is the heart ...
When those words left her lips,
my sob could no longer remain silent
and was quickly joined
by my family's sorrow
and muted chest heaves.
The technician continued
to search earnestly
for the missing heartbeat.
My sister finally said—
Could you please stop?

Hairy Kari

A year ago
all the hairs
lingering
at the edges
of the sink
would have made me
blind with rage;
now I read them
like tea leaves,
our collected
DNA telling
the future
in the most
unexpected
way.

ALEATHIA DREHMER

dyad

the sheer hitler
of abuse
a man is capable of.

~

the neurotic strength
of women
to survive it
after driving him there
in the first place.

JUSTIN HYDE

Dear River

Dear River Phoenix,

I remain your biggest fan in Texas. When I was seventeen, I hung a poster of you on my bedroom door in Fredericksburg, where various football players called me "skank" and said they would rather fuck a dog than fuck me. I was a virgin until I was 22. This is uncommon, especially in 20th-century Texas. I am now living in 21st-century Texas, and things are much the same—only more so. I enjoyed you in *Stand By Me* and *The Mosquito Coast*. When I think of you, I think of you as a boy saying, "Not if I see you first." Your delivery slayed me. You were so young but so old, so pure in your intensity. I would have eaten vegetables with you and watched your fingers fumble across the guitar strings. You remain my favorite Virgo male. I have a Virgo moon and ascendant. Also. My sun and Venus are conjunct in the house of Virgo, so my Virgo influence is considerable. As the calendar years accumulate, a woman becomes more like her sun and less like her moon, so these days, I am less the tongue-tied virgin (I still have my awkward moments, and I still hear every word a lover doesn't say.) and more the ranting and raving lunatic water bearer with one foot in the Rio Grande and the other foot on Jupiter. I've got God all over my toes, and I am dying in the throes of the most passionate love of my life at the redolent age of forty. I still haven't seen *My Own Private Idaho*, but I will. I know this is an important item to cross off the list. This morning, I watched the sunrise in Eagle Pass, Texas. I told my boyfriend I prefer fat, lazy tongue, and he said he will let the bees sting his tongue. Bees follow him everywhere he goes. He's a Capricorn, so he is always teaching me stuff. He has a Taurus moon, so as you can imagine he is one tactile, stubborn, stuck-in-his-ways motherfucker. Also. His Mars in Sagittarius adores my Venus in Aquarius. He grills red meat for me. I love red meat, but I might have given it up for you. Would you have given up the drugs for me? I wouldn't have asked you to. I'm writing this from a starry, misty distance. Reality can be so stark, quite the wake-up call, so much cold water splashing on your dreaming face. You never know if it will work with someone until you are sharing a cheap motel room, braving your way in the dark past the tiptoeing-on-eggshells phase. There are so many ways to give and receive love and so many variations and so many thrilling combinations, and I am still a sexual apprentice. I am not immune to infatuation, but I've put away the camera and the candy cane, because I'm in it now, the rapturous sea, where I am mermaid, and he is blue whale, and we are singing past the stinging phase. Really, I don't know what else there is. Well, breakfast, sure ... forks, dirty dishes, the budget, credit cards, road trips to San Antonio, angry relatives, long lines at the post office, and death at the end, smirking. Now, I'm thinking of Johnny Cash ... your brother as Johnny Cash. He did a great job. Reese was cute, but I don't think she earned that Oscar. I am still practicing my acceptance speech. Someday I will star in a movie of my life, because I don't think Kristen Stewart could quite pull it off. My boyfriend is always saying he'll see various women in Heaven. His ex-wife, The One That Got Away ... and me. If Heaven isn't a dive bar with blue Xmas lights and a jukebox fat with Johnny Cash, Townes Van Zandt, Daniel Johnston, Billie Holiday, Patsy Cline, Led Zeppelin, King Tuff, White Fang, Destroyer, The Church, and Elvis (one of the greatest Capricorns ever), I'd prefer to stay dead, thanks. But if the eternal dive bar does in fact exist, I will see you there, and the first hundred rounds are on me, sweet man. My McDonald's coffee is getting cold, and now, it is time to dodge traffic and make my way to the nail salon. Pretty nails are still somehow important.

Love,
Misti

Pretty, Isn't It?

LAWRENCE GLADEVIEW

betty said
buttoning up
her blouse
&
looking out
the window

sure is doll
i replied
buckling
my belt

you
going to
be okay
the rest
of the
trip hun?
she
asked me
touching up
her lipstick
in
the mirror

betty
if i need you
i'll be sure
to hit
the button
i said
as i
stepped
around
her
out of
the
bathroom
& back
to
my seat.

Choice

"You spoil me;" she states,
"I feel guilty about that."
She slinks up to me, wraps her arms
around my neck.
For some strange reason, I'm speechless,
even after all these years.
She kisses me, then explains how
the new air conditioner she bought
(that we don't really need
and can't really afford)
is being delivered on Tuesday.
"You're too good to me," she adds,
as she slips from the room
as smoothly as she slipped in,
and I'm thinking,
What choice do I have, really?
I mean, just look at her!
What choice do I have
in anything, really—what?

MICHAEL ESTABROOK

Wind Through the Trees ...

HOSHO McCREESH

And it's always meant
something profound and
important to me—

       proud limbs
bent
by some terrible swell,
some ruthless
       and unseen force,
       the wise legs writhing, giving,
       the wise roots tangled deep down
       and clinging to the damp,
       black earth.

Always I thought
there was a lesson it in—

       something about
       patience,
       determination,
       a quiet
       perseverance.

But it wasn't until
just this second
(all the years
up 'til now
wasted)
that I realized
I'm not the
old, wise tree—

I've no style or grace
        while outlasting struggle,
        no Zen calm in these
        furious aerial tides—

            No, oh no, no, no …

I am the
ignorant, fugitive wind,

the thing
everything else
is made to
suffer.

Featured Writer

Sean Brendan-Brown

SEAN BRENDAN-BROWN

is a graduate of the Iowa Writers' Workshop. A medically retired Marine, he is the author of three poetry chapbooks (*King of Wounds*; *No Stopping Anytime*; and *West Is a Golden Paradise*), a fiction chapbook, *Monarch of Hatred*, and a short-story collection, *Brother Dionysus* (MilSpeak Books). He has been published in *Notre Dame Review*, *Wisconsin Review*, *Indiana Review*, *Texas Review*, *Southampton Review*, and in the University of Iowa Press anthologies: *American Diaspora* and *Like Thunder*. He is the recipient of a 1997 NEA Poetry Fellowship and a 2010 NEA Fiction Fellowship. He currently lives in Olympia, Washington, and can be found at is.gd/facebookSBB.

Zealots

Trust is treasure—poorly
repaired masonry reflects a face—
the last rotted Salvation Army
chest spills its coins into the abyss;
say the face is Mary's; she's worth
more than doubloons, cut-rate
angel in the sun, all that's left
of our holy-war wall; cease-fire
fascinating, though the sculpture's
crude. Where I wait, love is dead,

the unclean warm air, quiet—
pride and sin took it all away
& now, I know God for what is
kind—a final hour, anticlimax partakers,
or a duel's resolution when both fire
unscathed or both topple and die.
Evil avails its worshippers in happy
termination; joss-stick fingers

knead supplication, pay
without ceasing for forgiveness;
ne m'arrête pas, fantôme odieux:
pass, despicable phantom; surrender
your zinc bucket of angels writhing
on brass treble-hooks. Dawn rubs
our faces in a century of fled dreams.

SEAN BRENDAN-BROWN

Ramble Tamble

*(mud in the water, roach in the cellar, bugs in
the sugar —CCR, "Ramble Tamble")*

SEAN BRENDAN-BROWN

Answer your own question, silly little
dark-master prince: what does darkness
have to do with you, or mastery?
Fool.
Good thing it isn't Christmas anymore,
Tupac sings remix: *pickie me up*
wakie me up; 3 a.m., we talk 'til dawn—
everything from the prez to Christ: you
believe; I don't. For Halloween,
let's be Osama and the camel,
twist li'l flags around our heads
like helicopters!

We've got it bad, no phones: hang
up, call right back was our life. Fool.
Out with someone, kept thinking
about someone else: Happy Teriyaki,
breath like egg roll plum-syrup,
tongue swimming in that sweet
hot soy saucy mouth, brain thinking
about someone else. Fucker swearing

in Chinese 'cause I don't like french
fries all middle-frozen; just fry 'em some
more! Freshman in the corner fumbling
chopsticks, squashes yellow zits, checks
the pus on his finger; gal-pal drops her fork,
Gross! You see in her face all she wants
is better than this clown. Says it loud
like his mom: *do something* about your face,
but what can he do? Not getting any,
he resorts to puerile grossness: men never
learn, and that's a compliment.

96

Ten Thousand Shields & Spears

SEAN BRENDAN-BROWN

The VA surgeons finished
my father with a genre of cuts.
I lit his cigarettes below scarlet keloids—
humor still in him,
he wrote, *Someday these really will kill me.*
His last request was cremation,
so cancer would know fire.

When it was over, I took him to the place
of burning, listened to the roar of furnace.
I shook his can of ashes into Lake Michigan.
Fragrant diesel lapped them up, & I prayed,
"Earth, reassemble him with pig-iron
bones, draw his heart in quartz."

My father loved winter, laughed
at my ineptitude with cold's rules—
my inability to fix, with a slap, the radio.
Today, ice closed Cedar River, ten thousand
spears rattled glass shields. If this shack had
value, I'd buy my way warm.

Santa's coming, the TV warns: another sad
quarrel; trees stripped, scabrous rose petals heaped.
Expect ice, Dad's radio gloats. I switch it off,
vacuum tubes exhale
heat onto the bullseyes of my palms.

The radio doesn't speak anymore,
and as Dad's not here to fix it, so it remains—
hot box tick-ticking, without news.

Pro Bono Publico

SEAN BRENDAN-BROWN

*("Thus, little by little, I became conscious
where I was; my infancy died long since,
and I live."* —St. Augustine)

Place me in a quiet, gambrel-roofed parsonage
painted white w/blue trim & set so far back
from the gate
it disappears into roses, elms, & Lombardy
poplars, where the clamor & infection
of innovation is powerless.

America, where all things flourish but genius:
the extended British Empire senile & fat; soil
fertilized with Native blood, slave's sweat,
and West Indian rum—I plant a garden to soothe
the spirits
and an orchard, though I'll be old when it bears.

This morning, a crow gobbles the Turkey figs,
a bus sluicing through mist spooks him, & he hops
about, rotted fig dripping from his beak. Forgive
my bitterness; it'll pass with the rain. The harvest
I await
is a renaissance—these dark ages shall brighten.

This republic of the setting sun will be reborn:
a congregation of astronomers shall lead us
into the sky.
I'm preparing for the pageant, jarring strawberry
preserves from bought strawberries; the crows
can keep the figs. My pride is for the people I love.

Power

I first kissed you in shadow,
orange sundown outside
the condemned graystone church—
touch intensified by summer's end—
right to go with you, so I went.

We stitch our happiness to rotted
fabric, bruised calm. Make me God, it'd
be different—my world unaffected
by disease, corruption, war, greed,
hunger. A stupid thing to say;

they'd destroy that deity,
cage its angels, dismantle its humane
temples. So, build me a castle forty feet
higher—I'm too well after falling.
Power isn't money, position, class,

or rebellion: it's rising Tuesday
to assume your humble desk,
announcing, *I'm no longer dying*.
They don't believe it but are glad
down in the valley, the valley so low.

SEAN BRENDAN-BROWN

Bush Ducks Shoes

The insult in Arabic is *ibn al-kundara*: son of a shoe. It's an ancient way to vent frustration.

True, Muntazer al-Zaidi flung clean Oxford wingtips at the enemy he thought beneath him, as low as shoes.

In Bedouin days, the missile would have been a sweaty, camel-dung-drenched slipper: mortal insult to have so

foul a gauntlet dashed in one's face. Bush ducked: the president was always very adept

at ducking—no harm done, the world belly-laughed heartily before the crash.

SEAN BRENDAN-BROWN

Earth Never Whimpers Per Person

SEAN BRENDAN-BROWN

The remote and faithful light of stars—
so old, they die as we finally see
them—light passing through time
when God first toyed with Adam—
serving up their heads on silver patens;

out of everything there ever was,
does anything last? I don't know,
but I search: it's a fulfilling
life, an Icarus who can swim.
The odor of age is oil—it curses

those who rob its tombs, it kills
the air—coal and gas are fireflies
whose burst guts illuminate
our fingers: power chattel,
mankind rides, brain a black seed.

Earth will be fine, never whimpers
per person. An eldritch stain
for sundown, what lovely effects.
And infection, languid in its fleshy
troves, so romantic, sailors of the sky.

Another Birthday

SEAN BRENDAN-BROWN

Flipping
through the Wichita Falls Coyotes high
school yearbook: there's what's-her-name,
the girl you swore you'd love 4-ever;
there's Johnny "da Bull" Burke—
so big, so tough,
who punched nose-blood
all over your KISS Army T-shirt.

Sonofabitch—
how you flew home from Pendleton
after Marine boot to square the past,
bumped Johnny at Kroger: he
didn't recognize you. Followed him
to the parking lot where da Bull (balding,
still pimpled, fat, thick glasses sunk
into the pug nose, pregnant wife cursing
the heat) stumbled, ding-ding bounced
a can of chili. And their car—battered '77
Ford Maverick—where's Johnny's '69 Z28?

How
beat he looked, how pathetic
the dangling Playboy air-
freshener. He drove
away, stealth-drinking
Miller, wife cursing,
pulling Ritz from
a box.

THE LUMINAIRE AWARD

HONORABLE MENTION

2013

BEST POETRY

*Lo*ve Penned Red

My mother finished her life in side-boxes
in shabby playhouses; she was an actress,
and then she was old, and then she watched.

She had Old World grace and cut fresh flowers
each morning for Sebastian, an octogenarian who
brought ice-cold four-percent milk in bottles.

She'd laugh at this theater—lighting wrong,
music wrong, set design some novice's concept
of angst, the discomfort of a crowd

smelling each other's cured flowers,
exhaust from the organ snuffing candles, souring breath.
Everyone thinks someone else

has ruined the tempo—she'd take responsibility,
wave off-white and marble-veined hands thumbs-up,
airbrushed blue mouth whistling

to silence that freaky, cheap-tuxedoed
impresario licking beads of sweat from his Cupid's bow
and patting the coffin lid like a sideboard

he's left a deck of cards on, or his gloves.
She'd hand him a summons, *love* penned red.
That'd do it; God willing, she'd be his halting place.

SEAN BRENDAN-BROWN

Crows

SEAN BRENDAN-BROWN

When I was a boy
everyone shot crows—
God-given right—
though I was sorry

for them, I thought them
malevolent, too, all black
& bloody. One night, Dad
brought home six babies,

caged them with plywood,
staples, and chicken-wire.
The crows made no noise.
I fed them toast & scraps;

the cage remained a week,
then suddenly, it was empty—
I pressed my face into wire—
the screen smelled of crow, rust,

bread, and bacon drippings.
Released, they must have cawed
excitement; I envied their wings,
their undisguised hatred & committed

cold black eyes that held my own
when I fed them peanuts. They
scorned my sympathy and jabbed
my fingers without apology.

Rotating Home on Emergency Leave

DAVID S. POINTER

The Deputy Provost Marshal at rotation end
always extorting automobiles
from lower-ranking service
members for resale
                threatening legal hold or
remote duty station   relocation.

My grandfather is terminal with cancer,
and I'm going to skull fuck the deputy
military police director if he presses the
issue, as I'm needed elsewhere, and he's
not getting my car for $15.00.
He comes to understand this, and I fly out
on emergency leave, having to outmaneuver
a captain trying to bump me for his own
rest-and-relaxation flight.

We watch him explode like old ordnance
as Kadena Airport staff escort him away,
and he'll have to be content with earlier
orders for jungle warfare school and two
other highly desirable training assignments
that he took from me to bestow on Marines
in his own unit, as I fly for final days with my
grandpa, where I impersonate a loving human
being, just in from the land of a few good men.

Near to Him

CHARLES P. RIES

T he cranberry swamp was just below our farm. It was usually filled with low-lying water and an abundance of cattails. Blackbirds lived and nested there, as well as countless rabbits. It was five acres in diameter, with a murky pool at the center where muskrats built their hutches. In the dead of winter, we'd go ice skating, swerving and weaving our way in and out of the cattails and around the muskrat hutches. At the north end of the swamp was a small, wooded area filled with boxelder saplings. My father called them *weeds of the forest* because they grew fast and in just about any condition, including in those of a swamp.

We never walked in the swamp until it froze over in early winter. But this autumn, after a particularly dry summer, we found ourselves being able to run through it and play hide-and-seek in it. My eleven cousins, who lived nearby, and my siblings would play war by pulling off the tops of cattails and using them to beat each other over the head, sending plumes of cottony seedlings into the air. It was a natural playground with unending things to see and experience.

Pheasant hunting season began in late fall. Most of the cornfields had been harvested by this time, and the birds were fat from dining under apple and cherry trees and eating corn dropped by the combines. It was one brilliant, clear day in autumn. The sky was bright blue, and the landscape burst with fall colors. The second round of chores was

THE LUMINAIRE AWARD

HONORABLE MENTION

2013

BEST PROSE

over, and, as I was walked through the feed house, I found my father loading his 22-rifle.

"Let's go hunting," he said, looking up at me.

"What?"

"Hunting, in the swamp. I set up a blind. Let's get some pheasants."

My older siblings had already gone into the house for the day—it would just be the two of us.

My father and I walked to the bottom of the mink yard, hopped the guard fence, and walked another hundred yards through towering cattails toward the center of the swamp. The ground was uncharacteristically firm and easily held both of us. My father had come down earlier in the week and piled a few old, wooden fence posts into an informal barrier for us to hide behind. Along with his rifle, he'd brought a burlap bag filled with cobs of dry seed corn.

As he settled in behind the blind, he told me, "Take this and dump it about two hundred feet up ahead. Just dump it in one big pile and get back here. We'll see who's hungry today."

I did as he told me and ran back with the empty burlap bag flying behind me, jumping over the blind and settling in beside him.

"Don't talk. Don't move. Just watch the corn pile," he said.

We lay on our bellies and watched the center of the swamp bed where he had told me to place the corn. His rifle rested on one of the posts, and we waited for the birds to find the corn. I never got this physically close to my father. I don't remember him ever hugging me or directly talking to me, other than to give me reprimands or directions about work. But on this sun-drenched afternoon in the heart of the cranberry swamp, I lay perfectly still and soaked in the odor of his work clothes. I listened to the slow, steady rhythm of his breathing and inhaled the aroma of his Blue Boar pipe tobacco.

The cattails swayed to a breeze that blew out of the southwest. The air was dry and warm, and the low hum of insects slowly lulled me into sleep, when the *crack* of my dad's rifle shook me awake.

"Got him! Hustle out there, and grab it," my father ordered in a loud whisper.

My father's 22 was precise and quiet. With a scope mounted on its barrel, it was deadly accurate. Unlike a 12-gauge shotgun that blew birdshot, the 22 shot small bullets. Because of its relative silence, it didn't scatter other birds that might be hiding nearby. Rather, they'd sit tight and, once the coast was clear, begin to move and return to the pile of corn.

I ran out, grabbed the bird, and hustled back to the blind, placing it between my father and me as we resumed our vigil. This time, I kept my eyes open. In about fifteen minutes, a few more birds appeared, circling the corn pile and feeding. My father took aim at the rooster with its distinctive red-ringed neck and nailed him, again telling me to run and get it. We recommenced our waiting, and my father soon laid out his third bird for the afternoon. By the end of our two hours together, we'd bagged three hens and two roosters with five clean shots.

"That'll do it. That's pretty damn good. We're going to be eating some pheasant. Let's head back before your mom thinks we got lost."

We worked our way back through the cattails. I walked behind, carrying the five birds in the burlap bag, while my father carried his rifle. We hopped back over the guard fence and walked to the carpenter shop, where my father quickly and efficiently cleaned the birds. We then went into the house for dinner.

At the kitchen table that evening, my father, true to form, didn't say much about our time together other than, "It went well. We were lucky to get five birds," before returning to his meal.

Knowing she wasn't going to get much information from him, my mother turned to me and asked, "Well, did you have fun with your dad, Chucky? What was it like hunting for pheasants? Was it exciting?"

Like my father, I was taciturn in my reply and gave my mother a minimum of, "Yup, I had fun, Mom; we got five birds." I had to fight myself to keep from saying more. I wanted to shout and tell everyone how great it was to be with my father, to lie next to him in a pheasant blind, and how proud I was to be his son. I wanted to tell them what a perfect day it had been and that I wanted one hundred more just like it, but I knew that if I said it, I would break the spell and lose him forever. I wanted to tell them I was afraid he'd evaporate like mist in the morning sun if I adored him too much. So there at the dinner table, I became nothing. I didn't express my excitement or publicly adore my father. I tried to be silent, stoic, and numb. Like him, I ate with my head down and shoved my feelings to the floor. I strangled the ball of joy that was rising up in me. I chewed my food and concentrated on becoming like him, because I knew that if I could become like him, it would bring me more days like today.

Cassette Tapes

WILLIAM TAYLOR, JR.

I was young but old enough
to know I wouldn't always be,
and it was, say, a Saturday night in
Bakersfield,
maybe summertime,
my old Datsun parked behind a Safeway
or some other place
the cops didn't go.
I was maybe with a friend
and there was music,
there was always music,
cassette tapes playing
from a portable thing
tossed in the back,
and we had a six- or a
twelve-pack of something,
and we listened and drank
and sang
and talked a bit now and then,
usually about a girl,
there was always a girl,
and outside the darkness
was a palpable thing,
but the darkness could go to hell
because we had the drink and the music,
and we already knew that life
wouldn't hold
much more for us
than this,
and that just made us sing
all the more.

Any god worthy of the name

D. A. PRATT

Any god
worthy of the name
would have absolutely no need
for worship.

Absolutely none.

Surely, this is self-evident.
This *must* be self-evident.
Why isn't this self-evident?

Bookseller to the CashWrap

CEE

Bluh
Bluuuuhh
B*luhhuh*h
BLuhh, bluhhhHHhhhuhhhh-BlUH
BluHH
Bluh-Bluh-Bluh-Bluh-Bluh-Bluh-Bluh-Bluuu—
BLUUUUUUHHHDDDDD—ehehhhhhh ... *ehn* ... dd!!
Yeah?
What else?
Thanks, no
Sounds nothing
I'll pass
Oh, Stephen King wrote it?
Okay

Alarmed in
Space

(for Lori Janies)

HARRY CALHOUN

My friend Lori takes a photo of a sign
outside a room filled with art: *"Do not attempt*
to enter this room after business hours.
This space is alarmed." Shortly after, I comment
on my chronic fear of heights, and Lori says,

"Harry is alarmed in space." And indeed I am,
not lost in space, but alarmed. Our whole society
these days is nounedly verbed: The space is alarmed,
our interests are leveraged, at Christmas we're gifted,
at work we're tasked, to get ahead we're advantaged,
and to sum this up, let me nutshell it for you.

Most of you listening to me read this
or reading it on the page might not understand,
and this is not condescending, simply the drift
that the outrigger of language has gone through.
We have become so languid in our journey,

the usage has become so imprecise, that the GPS
is our soul, the map means little and the memory nothing.
Reading sentences of imprecise tripe feels like sitting
in a room filled with cigar smoke with a tiny feather
tickling the back of your neck. Or forced up the dizzying
skyscraper hung by a hangnail, alarmed in space and panicked.

She was one
of those

ALAN CATLIN

dressed-in-black,
fool-for-love kind of
wannabe poets, burned
out in her twenties, all
of her heroes dead like
Dylan Thomas—her, too,
by drowning, long-legged
bait, rings on her bare toes,
waiting for a nibble.

Whatever Happened to Nellie?

PAULA ANNE YUP

Back to her gray rainy country
after violence done to her by a boy
so I read in the paper
how my monkey friend
last seen at a goodbye party in spring
has flown this chicken coop island in summer
and I'm left with the confetti
old poems she wrote
her wild wild ways
diving deep into the lagoon
singing karaoke in nightclubs
her boyfriend some call a thief
just the memory sliced thin
her posh accent her curly hair
tall tales which may or may not
have held water

Polska

Polska, he blurted, face full of marvel and
    mirth
at the irony of the land of my mother's
    birth.

Polska, his deep, slow grumbling
shook me to my feet,
a tank across my terrain, rumbling
a love letter piercingly sweet
from the mouth of a Saturday Night Special.

He studied my face gazing back at him, proud.
Chin up, Girl, don't give this man any ground.

Polska, my mother always said,
"Never show a man your whole ass."
What could that mean?
Never show a man your ass whole?
What could happen?

What cheek to turn?
What cleft to cover?
What cleavage to close?

Why the ass?
Why not the breasts?
Questions you dare not ask
your mother, or her guests.

Oh, *moja matka,* if only I knew
how to discern your advice.
Had you not been so cryptic,
you might have spared
his five o'clock shadow,
my Sssinnabar lipstick.

Why not just tell me what'd make him
click his heels *Jawohl*,
bend his steely spine over mine,
melt his thighs till he kneels,
part his smile for my bite,
offer his boyish neck
till he purrs with delight
at each lick and each peck,
waving his banner, white
with such brave surrender
no general could ever tender.

Mama, you ironed my sheet
when we had no heat.
Now his smile warms me, quivering like soft whips,
little love flames flicking at my back.
But wait! He bridles, casting his smile in total eclipse.
Look, Ma, he knows how to cover his ass
better than I do. What class!

If I am so bold and so naughty,
perhaps he should take me over his knee,
slap me until he leaves a tattoo
of his palm, now so red and haughty.

In my perfume
he surrenders again.
Oh, what creatures
are these men?
Ist das a mann?

I was *born with white paper*
that his eyes sear blue words upon.

Polska, he murmured,
voice gone hoarse and husky,
eyes gone deep and dusky,
Ich küsse Ihre Hand.

Lithium Ashes

(for Julia)

ANGIE TURNER JEFFREYS

Again, it's the era of selfish martyrs. The
suicides cry from trees, fall with timbre
requiems, puddling on the leaves, the nooses,
collapsed ladders or broken branches. Shoes
fall like fruit beneath the Tree of Strategy and
Exit,

shrapnel from the outer space beneath their
feet, un-leapt, swaying from trees like sloths
and hate crimes. These are the voodoo-hoodoo
heroes, prayer candles lit in flaming honor.
Angry ghosts

for the angry hosts, they do
invoke spirits, bottle them out of bodies burned
in the crematory, unclaimed, souls caged:
another man bakes back to dust. Yahweh said to me
yesterday, the ovens

never should've gotten involved. Suicides slither on the
floor: I stand on my ladder, but I wear no noose. I
sleep and dream in terror that the dead will rise. But Yahweh
said he doesn't like the worms for tears of those who fought

not. He prefers red wine and blood asleep on altar before
the slaughter. Yahweh donates it all to the Red Cross.
But what about the suicides? Yahweh said they are the
walking dead. Aren't they burned and sprinkled out

like offerings? Yahweh replies, "Scattered like mustard
seeds." The Holy Ghost, though, can't grasp Band-Aids
with frankincense fingers frowning in the doorway. He said

don't mention the blood donations; it's too awkward to
explain. Yahweh left, a ghost behind a haze of face.

How and What

GEORGE HELD

How retrieve
What we receive
And lose?

No reprieve
For those
Who just grieve.

What we weave
Or conceive
All goes,

I believe,
In throes
On death's eve.

Unpacking

from
their
camping
trip

roy
& pam
watched
their
neighbor
joe
bring
home
flowers
to his wife
janice

man
it's been
a while
since
i did
that for
you
roy
said

i know
pam
replied

LAWRENCE GLADEVIEW

that's why
it's
been
a while
since i
did
to you
what
janice
& i
learned
at her
bachelorette
party.

The Father

*("One must have a mind of winter …
and have been cold a long time"*
—Wallace Stevens, "The Snow Man")

ANGELA CONSOLO MANKIEWICZ

Considering my dwelling place, my father
supplied me with a stoic's heart and made me
untouchable.

He knew there is only one way out
for someone like me: an end to the childhood
I suspected I was living,

release from the frenetic flailing trapped
inside me, swelling my limbs, thickening my
    tongue;
an aftertaste of sand.

Ah, yes, my father, perceptive "in his
    generation,"
knew an end to childhood could mean,
perhaps, an easier time of it for me,

an appreciation for the distinct pleasures
of dead-end sensation. Possibly,
not guaranteed, he would have warned,

if he'd dare to speak. And if he dared,
he would have said: Sit with folded hands
while the years pass;

in the meantime, do what they tell you
as much as you can, and don't say much; few
will notice until you've grown up;

even then, they will only throw up their hands
at the swollen limbs you've broken off
and left scattered about.

Nothing to be done about it, my father
would have said, I've done everything
I could; you must

gather yourself up now and run away
with as much of you
as you can find.

Mutha's Boy

TRAVIS TURNER

"**L**oad him up on the stretcher," the gruffy paramedic snorted, as he took a deep breath to lift the body. "Sonuvabitch is heavier than he looks."

The ancient, speckled skin—tan from days spent laboring in his garden—was now as cold as the Alabama summer would allow it be. Old Joe, not made for this world, finally went home. His old soul now rested with the love of his family, especially his dear mother.

"Mutha, can you help me tie this?" Joe shouted down the hallway, tussling with the silken fabric, careful not to tie it until the knot was pristine. As a young man, his will was undeniable. A fire drove him to succeed, to make his mother proud. He was well respected as a young scholar, a member of the debate club, and even the first initiate in his local fraternity, making him an accomplished young man, by all means. He was the first man in his family to go to college. All that was lacking was the most important emotional interest of all: love.

"I grabbed the eggs from the henhouse before we leave for service, Mutha!" Joe said, placing the eggs on the kitchen counter.

"Son, you've got this all knotted up. Let me give it a woman's touch."

"Mutha, what am I ever going to do without you? I swear I'd be half dead in a ditch somewhere, if it weren't for you."

"Don't forget to zip your pants, Joseph."

After college, Joe couldn't leave. He stayed behind in the sleepy town to look after his mother and the family homestead. He had never known his father. The faceless prick had left before Joe was old enough to walk. Rumors swirled that the old man was a drunk, and abusive to Joe's mother. Joe, however, had never met the patriarch of the York family.

Whenever Joe was asked about his father, Joe's reply was always the same, "Mutha said he left before I could show him how to be a real man!"

Eventually, Joe took a good-paying job with the county and became more of a staple in the community. He led church hymns, discussed local politics over bourbon and cigars, even became an advisor to several campus organizations at his alma mater, in order to give back to those who nourished him in his early days. Despite a close call or two, Joe remained a lifelong bachelor. Instead of running the streets late at night like a spring chicken, Joe would be seen driving his sweet Mutha to church each Sunday or taking her out to lunch at one of the quaint cafés littered in between storefronts downtown. Joe was a good, attending son.

No one expected Mutha to live as long as she did, so it was no surprise when she went face down in her plate at the dinner table. Some said her longevity was due solely to Joe's love for his mother. Others said it was because if she had kicked it, the boy would've been as lost as a lamb. Most agreed that Joe could never get out from under Mutha's wing. Joe liked it there, safe from the cruel realities of the world surrounding him. When she did finally pass at age 91, Joe was a man high in age himself. He was now 64 and a retired homebody. The love of his life now taken from him, all that was left for Joe was to withdraw.

"Taken too soon," he said at the funeral service, as somber tears of passion trickled down the side of his spectacles.

Noticeably shaken, Joe wasn't seen for close to two weeks. Neighbors and friends alike called and brought dishes, only to leave them on his doorstep after minutes of knocking and calling for the old man. The phone rang off the hook for days straight, but no Joe. Not even a peep from Mutha's baby bird. The concern grew, and eventually, one of the local sheriff's deputies stopped by with the local pastor, after Joe didn't show up for service for three straight Sundays. Suicide was the latest gossip. What they found startled them both.

Upon entering the old revival-style home, the stench hit them immediately. Unmistakable to the lawman, the house reeked of rotting meat. The Father pulled his shirt collar over his nose to keep from tossing the potluck supper in his belly.

As they made their way into the living room, they noticed the house was in immaculate condition, except for the nauseating smell. Throw pillows left on each side of the sofa, a throw blanket folded up neatly, and remote controls side by side on the coffee table.

The kitchen told another story. One of a half-finished meal. Two places were set, with candles in place on each side of a floral porcelain vase overflowing with dead daisies, crumbling off of their stems. Two wine glasses sat on the table. One full—one empty, with cherry-red lipstick stains on the outer rim. The bone-china plates told a similar story. One sat with portions still in place, perfectly intact, and the other, only containing a chicken breast and wing, nearly picked clean.

Creak crack creak crack creak crack. As they further explored the untouched refuge, the lawman noticed subtle sounds coming from one of the back rooms.

"Father, I hope this ain't messy," the deputy said.

As the door eased open, the smell became more intense, like that of month-old carrion casserole. Lying there, face down on the comforter, was Joe's body, lifeless, as a machine continued to thrust in and out of his backside. The contraption was some sort of sex device and was still running, though not at full throttle. On the bed next to Joe, lay dozens of home pictures, pornographic in nature, featuring Mutha and her teenage son. The soft repetition of Glen Campbell's "The Hand That Rocks the Cradle" creeping adrift from Joe's stereo added to the uneasiness of the two men's revelation.

The cock crowed three times from the backyard, as the ambulance arrived to cart off the body, now fully concealing the cherry-red lipstick, fishnet stockings, and high heels.

"Heart attack," the EMT said, loading the body.

Neighbors stood along the curb, speaking somewhat courteously, mainly curiously. "Such a shame," and "Must've been hard for him to deal with her loss," the onlookers said softly amongst themselves. The cock crowed again. "Well, at least he's roosting at home now, enveloped in his Mutha's love."

a sense of place: streetwalking

under the Parthenon
streets stretch broad
narrow   arced dark   bricked   cobbled
stones of rivers   Rush Street   Rue des
Capucines   the Reeperbahn
past the Plaka   Plaza del Sol   Place Pigalle
Saint Pauli   Alexanderplatz   polinische
sputtering mist
golden mannequins in golden windows
winos lying in blind alleys
Unter den Linden   the rain
cold as the last man's bones

ROBERT SCHULER

Unprovoked

Sitting on that hard, cold, unfinished floor
The simplicity of an egg salad sandwich
And its side bag of chips
Masquerades as a culinary delicacy
On a construction site that is tough enough
Without ... Him
Like a Brahmin to a street beggar
Standing at my feet
Peering down from his height
Lighting and inhaling
His cigarette
Then
Pointing at my lunch, declaring
"That shit will give you a heart attack"

DENIS SHEEHAN

Cousin Drunkus Returns (drunk tricks)

CEE

I don't want to go out anymore
I like my trailer home
Or, I did before here you were
Wanting to drink in my home
Wanting to use one of my glasses
Which I have to retrieve
By standing in front of you
Waiting for you to finish
Which you wouldn't do
Without finishing,
Going to give me my glass several times
Like a gas station drinking bird
The
Swwiiiiiinng, WHIP!, into
Backward for another draught
I want that glass
It's my glass
My stepfather paid for it, and I need
To wash it out

Somewhere parallel to the Cream City Collective

FRANKIE METRO

you sit
with your knees touching
and feet apart,
across from a parking garage
where I am pissing
on the dank wall inside,

where it smells like mildew
and motor oil,
grease tracks pooling near
the cracks
beneath a fishing boat
with rust on the lures
and blue felt in the seat.

When I emerge,
your knees point in
the other direction,
and your heels are
clicking while you
give me that smirk
that we know means
I actually did it,
and there's a strong
possibility someone
saw
the trail I left behind,

something yellow and caked
in mildew,

something that mingles with
the scent of motor oil,
rusty lures, and
blue felt.

When I sit next to you,
you giggle and point
to the couple on the balcony
above the garage,
laughing
and
pointing
in our direction,

and I suddenly realize
the boards over
my head
were not as thick
as I thought,

riddled with spying eyes
and cracks,

cracks big enough for
everyone to see
and smell
my everything,

as it runs off
into the gutter
at your shuffling feet.

You tell me
that you could see us
living in Milwaukee,
and I remind you about
the cold winters,

while the couple
overhead
make noises
we can't interpret ...

Revenge of the Alien Clockwork Nanobot Poet

CHRISTOPHER ROBBINS

He moved with funereal swiftness,
Attacked the mutant mindset of miniature Morths.
O woe! O heavenly celestial citadels
Of non-Earthly but similar-to-Earth Earthiness!

You are the growers of the wine. No, wait—
I mean, you are the Knowers of the Sign.

I am the God, with a capital G,
Of this Refurbished Clockwork Planet
Of misguided poet-martyr-warriors
With your rusted helioblimpers limping
Through the 64-bit encrypted atmosphere
Like two-bit nano-pirates.

The Great Wind-Down has begun.
I have sprinkled salt on the key
And swallowed it whole.

I have sent zombie were-mutants
To mow your lawns and to shine your shoes—
Oh, and to eat your children.

Dormant

Deep inside me
lives
a tiny, wild creature,
lambent,
waiting,
purring.

To quell that darling thing
would kill my essence.
So, shush, little one,
sleep.

Dream of your companion
to come
one night,
rampant,
stealthy,
inside you.

MERILYN JACKSON

Caring

JASON FISK

Weary winter air
cold concrete and asphalt
warm breath spilled from their mouths
heads exposed
whistling through red ears
The signal told them to walk
The woman grabbed the girl's hand
and started across
six lanes of road
The girl held her baby
doll by its hand
They crossed one lane
two lanes
three lanes
Then the woman picked up her pace
and the girl's arm pulled tight
displeasure molded her face
The doll slipped from the girl's hand
She broke from the mother's grip
and bent back to pick up the doll
The woman yelled
and pointed up at the blinking signal
re-grabbing the girl's hand
and dragging her to the curb
The girl held her baby
doll by its plastic foot
while its head dragged
and bounced across
the winter salt street
scuffing its plastic head

Out of the Flowerpot

A foot grew out of the flowerpot.
The foot was heavy and green.
The foot needed water to grow.
Hands started to grow out, too.
Rain fell gently. Soon, there was
a head growing out of the flowerpot.
Ears started to grow, and the mouth
from the head only spoke in French.

LUIS CUAUHTÉMOC BERRIOZÁBAL

D. H. Lawrence and *The Man Who Died*

ALAN CATLIN

("The dead have never bothered me. It is the living I fear." —Patricia Cornwell, *Postmortem*)

Escape is from the pits, black holes
of Birmingham, dark skies friezed by
smelter light, dense fogging smoke, rain
clouded by an acid wash, along deep-rutted,
rural roads, cindered paths, ash downs covered
by a grimy mist. Deep breathing is a wheezing
blood song eked from primogenative tubercular
lungs, an ode to mortality inscribed on foolscap:
After Imitations and Recognitioning by one
John Keats, esq. Wandering leads to quarry's
edge, derelict chalk mines, earth moved to make
cement, acres of residual dust, empty huts,
communal centers, workers' itinerant shacks
left empty when work stopped, equipment was
left to rust, the holes filled with a pasty
accumulation of rain, squalid breeding grounds
for insect larvae skimmed by oils, residues,
a legacy left by thieving landlords, robber barons
for those unable to move on, those cursed to have
contracted a post-industrial disease of seeing;
where a match strikes water, it burns.

Triggered

"I might be the pot calling the kettle black"
she said before yelling
"You shouldn't drink to forget ..."
She continued
and I began shuffling the photographs
of my memory
flip
   flip
      flip
         the black and whites
caressing the scar
There it is ...
cast iron on a wood-burning stove
bubbling moisture into the dry oaky air
inhaled before the scream
an arching silver handle and wouldn't you know
that damn black kettle

DENIS SHEEHAN

Not every bird can be a songbird

LEAH ANGSTMAN

The Western Island Scrub Jay
thrusts up his pretty blue
to caw and haw and hack and hem
and grated cackle spew.

From lusty beak, to tear the sky
with wincing, ugly flair,
without a song, he clatters on,
to let me know he's there.

I do not mind his hissing.
I do not mind his call;
for if it weren't for grated ear,
I'd not hear him at all.

Like perfume that must leave the nose
—Scent maddens that lingers long!—,
not every bird can be a songbird,
or we'd never hear the song.

All I can think and hope

MICHAEL ESTABROOK

Heading back home, finally, after 6 interminably
long days and nights away at yet another
supercilious, waste-of-time business meeting.
(All we have is time, isn't it?)

The shadow of the airplane follows along far below,
a dark, ghostly smudge sliding eerily
across the snowy landscape,
over fences and barns, rocks and roads,
cars and lakes and trees.

And all I can think about (as usual),
all I can picture in my mind (yes, yes, we know)
is me sitting on my heating pad,
watching my documentaries on TV,
sipping my beloved Starbuck's iced coffee—
my stunningly beautiful, sweet,
and radiant wife close by, where she belongs,
doing something or other on her iPad.

And all I can hope (beyond all hopes),
is that she is, indeed, still there
and hasn't yet run off
with that pesky lawn-care guy
with the big arms full of fuzzy tattoos.

Doppelgänger

SHAUNA OSBORN

My nocturnal self has left—
    lost her somewhere in Oakland
        to the blacktop-covered roads.

She feared the desert heat
after the coldness of the city.
    Feared it'd melt her resolution,
        drown out her loudest screech—
            replace the hard, coal-pressed hate
            that serves as her grounding center
            with a dripping puddle of snot.

While I wander the white & painted sand,
she frolics through asphalt & smog,
    roams among drag queens & junkies
    that ride the waves of Puget Sound—
        making love to dreadlocked poet beggars
        stealing rides on cable cars &
        slicing the leash off every dog she sees
            with her dad's rusty pocketknife.

Scott saw her late last week, flagged her down
from alternate subway platforms, screaming &
jumping like someone slain in the spirit,
    but the only response he received was a dramatic
    turn, her long braided dreads brushing the subway
    floor, as she bent in full curtsy &
    then a slow-blown kiss
    as she walked away.

Apologizing after sex (let's break this down)

All right
I can list about 3 things you're apologizing to her for
You either mean it or you don't mean it
If you mean it, you're gutless
Don't even talk to me, you're nothing
If you don't mean it, you're a most clever slave
All right
If you don't mean it and plan to do it again,
Vaya con Dios, muchacho
Just let me get out of the blast site, here
If you don't mean it, but actually Do feel
A certain responsibility
That you'll try very hard to work on, later,
Um
All right
Then, why didn't you mean it?

Either be selfish or be ashamed,
The two are oil and water; they don't mix
Selfishness Can't Be Ashamed
That's why it's Selfishness

An Inheritance

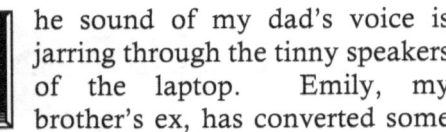

The sound of my dad's voice is jarring through the tinny speakers of the laptop. Emily, my brother's ex, has converted some old home videos into DVDs. My father, now dead, is playing with my nephew, Noah, just a toddler at the time this was recorded.

In the video, Dad is showing Noah some spinning tops that my father has collected from all over the world. A pine box that Dad constructed to hold them sits on the dining room table. Some of the tops are the size of coffee mugs; others, as small as thimbles.

There seems to be no common thread in the collection: wooden, plastic, painted, neon, antique, artisan, those that light when you spin them. Still another bears the Lucky Charms logo. Noah's father—my little brother, Gabbie—says over my shoulder that he loved to play with the tops as a small child. I watch in silence. This is the first time I have ever seen them.

Several of the small tops are spun in quick succession, their whirring punctuated by small talk in the background. My father looks directly at me through the camera's eye.

"I have no money, Gabbie. This is your inheritance." Dad laughs at his own joke.

Unlike Gabbie, I was not raised by our father. We lived together the first five years of my life, during the short time Dad was married to my mother. He visited with varying degrees of regularity during my preadolescence, but as I got older, he would disappear for long stretches, one of which lasted fourteen years.

Four hours after his death, a woman I didn't know called me from Bogotá, Colombia, to tell me of his passing. I nearly slammed on my brakes in the middle of the McKees Rocks Bridge, as she continued on in broken English to say it was a heart attack. Old wounds began to break open. Tears I didn't realize I would have for him began to flow.

Sadness, rage, neglect, distant joyous memories, and a love for him I could not seem to quit: these things are my inheritance. The rest spins dizzily inside me, faster than a top.

The Youths of Gainsborough Estate

K. M. DERSLEY

there are many who boast
the toughness of Greenwich Estate,
nor do I deny it. I've been on Greenwich
and smelled the gas reservoirs
when the cocks were turned.
those youths are tough, and I uphold
the claims of Greenwich,
but still I am staggered by the brawniness
of the paper-delivering, pipe-fitting,
grass-mowing, wood-planing youths
out of old Gainsborough Estate.

what shall Greenwich or anyone put up
against the best of Gainsborough?
they shall have to make long journeys
and take up every lead
to secure the finest athletes, Lotharios,
charlatans and polymaths
to set alongside those
who come from Gainsborough Estate.

I look over at Felixstowe and see nothing.
I look toward Woodbridge and see nothing,
but over in Ipswich I make out the shapes
of the bike-riding, tree-climbing, campfire-
kindling, river-swimming youths
of Gainsborough Estate.

I went to Tokyo to see the wrestlers
and to Californian cow palaces to watch
young'uns plaster themselves
to the backs of broncs and beeves,
but nowhere did I see such ball-
kicking, bat-swinging, chewgum-chewing
chick-chasing youths
as those on Gainsborough Estate.

I went to Baffin Island. I went to the Gobi,
where they played horse rugby
          with a sheep carcass—
nowhere did I meet
the Airfix-gluing, puncture-mending,
comic-swapping, apple-scrumping youths
such as are known on Landseer Road, yes,
Landseer Road, way over there
deep down in the heart
of old Gainsborough Estate.

Estimated Losses

ALEATHIA DREHMER

On the brink of death
laden with possibility's
name—life—something
coveted and created,
always chasing after
10 fingers
10 toes
1 smile
at
any cost.

She looks at me,
her face ashen with worry
that only comes on the
coattails of a dying life,
and tells me she doesn't
feel so well.

I try to hide my knowledge
from her, this knowing that
her belly is rising with blood
and faded dreams of motherhood,
now holding on by threads.

My hand touches hers,
understanding the chances
we'll take for sweet replications
of our love.

Letters Between a Man in Berlin and His Worried Mother

PATRICK KINDIG

Mom,

Stained glass windows still
greet the rising sun with red
and yellow comrades.

Thomas

Dear Thomas,

Icarus also
greeted the sun with eager
arms. Remember this.

Prefer the earth to the sky,
Mom

Featured Writer

DOUG DRAIME

Doug Draime

emerged as a poet, playwright, and short-story writer, in the literary 'underground' in Los Angeles in the late 1960's. His latest book is *More than the Alley*, a full-length poetry collection from Interior Noise Press. Draime has three chapbooks also available: *Los Angeles Terminal: Poems 1971-1980* (Covert Press), *Rock 'n' Roll Jizz* (Alternating Current), and an online chap, *Speed of Light* (Right Hand Pointing). Draime was awarded PEN grants in 1987, 1991, and 1992; and during the last few years, he has been nominated for several Pushcart Prizes. He currently lives in Medford, Oregon. You can find out more about him at is.gd/linkedinDraime.

Vortex
Crossing

I counted the steps of my childhood home
several years after it was sold and broken
up into apartments. I stood in front of the
house and counted 9 steps. I was 36 at
the time. Remembering at 16, lying drunk
one night on the top step like a dead alley
cat. I remembered, distinctly, waking just
before dawn and carefully counting 13 steps,
including the one I threw up on.

DOUG DRAIME

When I Was Preparing for War

DOUG DRAIME

I built my roads with an Army surplus shovel,
moved over the cast-iron
steel soldiers
and the cast-iron steel Jeeps and tanks
to my car pool
and shooting range
around the cherry tree in the backyard.
The barracks of old shoeboxes I placed
lined like houses in anywhere U.S.A.,
along the brick path to the garden.
I had a Daisy pump-action BB gun
that I kept inside the door
of the old barn, where the cats
and tools lived. Some days, I'd sit for
hours waiting
for the cats to wander over near
my military installation.
And I got one, *ping!*, on a rainy day in October.
But I only got one; after that, the cats
wanted nothing to do with me or my
war-making ambitions. I can't blame them; I was
a crack shot with that Daisy pump.
I had hit the cat—Fred was his name—on his left hind leg,
and he limped for months. Years later, I was drafted.
I trained with an M14 rifle
for the U.S. Army Infantry, and I would purposely miss
the targets or shoot all around them in
Basic Training.
I only qualified with that rifle because
the Army makes your life miserable
if you don't.
I qualified as a Marksman, the lowest rating ...
but only in reverence to old Fred.

Carnival Poem

DOUG DRAIME

It is useless to point out
the way gray
suddenly turned to brown
when I put my hand up her dress,
between her thighs
and rubbed there.
I say *useless to point out* because
when speaking of eyes,
there are times when people
listen, and they'll ask was I
sure her eyes were gray to begin with
when I put my hand up her dress,
between her thighs
and rubbed there,
or was I sure it was brown
they turned to, not just a faded gray?
Well, it wasn't just the eyes.
Her whole face altered like a funhouse mirror,
and her voice took on the sound of
a faraway whirl, and all I could hear
was the silhouette of her words,
please do it harder, please,
bouncing off the water in
the Tunnel Of Love
when I put my hand up her dress,
between her thighs
and rubbed there.

On Elvis Presley's Birthday

DOUG DRAIME

Snow is falling heavy in
Oregon right now, as it was
in Indiana that day when I was 13, when I
first heard Elvis sing "That's All Right, Mama"
at Joe's Record Shop on 2nd Street.
The snow, then was in near-blizzard
proportions, as I
stood inside the store
listening and watching through the
storefront window,
enormous flakes falling and
covering the sidewalk, street, and cars
like a thick blanket being woven.

But Presley disappointed me
when I saw his picture on
the sleeve that the record was in.
I had heard him singing before, over the radio,
from a station in Nashville,
and he sounded like
a black man to me.
Elvis ain't
no name for a white man!

Though, as I continued to
listen to him, a certain kind of pride grew in me,
for all of the mixed breed of Southern
and Southern-Midwestern
white boys, like ourselves,
locked-up in one form or another of
gray and dingy poverty,
living and dying in all of our
'heartbreak hotels.'

Now, 20 years after his death,
it seems the whole world, like the
Colonel, is selling him like a whore,
pimping him in the
lobbies of crass, cheap merchandise.
But back then it wasn't like
that. I carried that 45 RPM
record home,
like it was a rare and priceless treasure.
Knowing within me it was a sign,
a signal of change in me, in music,
in the world at large, in the universe of
perpetual movement and uncertainty.
I knew it was real revolution.

Something was established that would change
everything forever in my world.
Today, when I walked to my mailbox
in the snow, I saw my footprints there, but on
that day when I was 13, I wouldn't
have been shocked at all to have looked
down and seen only snow.

Unexpected Wonder of a Nipple Standing Alone

DOUG DRAIME

Baring one breast
with her

T-shirt pulled up,
her right nipple

dark brown and
erect.

Near the Borderline

DOUG DRAINE

The motel was on the
outskirts of a town
from a drunken
John Huston movie.

I remember the exact placement
of the 5th of Johnnie Walker Red,
sitting next to the glasses
on the nightstand, but I
don't remember her name.

Her eyes were light blue and like dimming
bar lights, flickering over my
shoulders, always looking at the
graying adobe.

I kept the TV on, and I must have
rolled 10 joints.

She liked it from behind, bent over the
metal desk,
those lovely shadow-eyes blinking on and off at
the walls.

She never smiled once and gave me
one-word answers to
my questions, only looking at me
when I turned away.

She didn't even look up
when I paid her $20 more than she
said she was worth.

Name-Dropping for a Deceased Wife

DOUG DRAIME

(For Beth Partlow-Draime)

I never thought I'd look back on
her in memory. She seemed so
fastened to her being and her
extraordinary perception
of the world! I watched her joy when she
read Joyce and Kafka,
Chandler and Hammett, or James Cain ...
and even William Morris
and Lovecraft. And the times she appeared
to be mesmerized by
Erik Satie and Brahms, Van Morrison,
and Leonard Cohen,
playing on our
boombox
as she tended
the tomatoes
and squash in
the garden behind our house in Echo Park.

And the many passionate and lazy afternoons,
her red hair entwined
through my fingers as I
held up each strand to
the sunlight
streaming through our
bedroom windows.

156

There were her cryptic
postcards from
across the U.S.
on the way home to see her folks
in Kokomo. The one from
a bus station somewhere
in Texas said simply,
"I'm just listening."

There is no getting away
from her courageous and
passionate struggle
to get the oppressed
Soviet Jews out
of Russia; and there
is a tree planted
for her
in Israel.

She made the *big time*
when her friend,
Si, published an article
about her in
the *L.A. Times*.
Boris Penson and Mikhail Baryshnikov are in her debt.

But mostly, I remember the way she held a
drinking glass full of Jameson whiskey
like it was a china teacup.
Every moment of those
three years
is somewhere in
my memory
like soft, gray rain
falling
inside
a perfect
white cloud.

Sometimes

DOUG DRAIME

sometimes it points to the sky
of blue, pointing like a bird
dog. sometimes it buries itself
deep in the nothingness
of political thinking. sometimes
it screams through the black,
black lies once told by you
and me. sometimes it just sits
there like J. Edgar Hoover
with a cheap tape recorder,
plotting your death. sometimes
it spends years adding up numbers
in an attempt to round off
infinity. sometimes it hides
in the couch with change
from hundreds of pockets.
sometimes it burns and burns
the trees we can't see the
forest for. sometimes
it runs like an out-of-control
driverless locomotive down a
steep mountain pass.
sometimes it stands trendy poets
up against the wall of
timeless literature and shoots them.
sometimes it lances boils on the
butts of opossums. sometimes it checks
into motels under the names of
Curly, Moe, and Larry. sometimes it
loves beauty for the right reasons.
sometimes it can name every
painting in the Art Institute of Chicago
blindfolded. sometimes it is impossible
to decode with extra-sensory perception
or any other kind of perception.
sometimes it breaks your heart. sometimes
it plans wars on planets in

distant galaxies. sometimes it
whittles exquisite little angels
out of cherry wood. sometimes it stands on
its head and imitates Erica Jong.
sometimes it captures butterflies,
then sets them free in the Pope's
bedroom. sometimes it goes into
tirades over the absurdity of
collective consciousness. sometimes it
teaches law students at Harvard how to make
tiny gas chambers. sometimes it stumbles around
in Dante's *Inferno*, selling copies of
Milton's *Paradise Lost*. sometimes it poses
as P. T. Barnum standing behind
a billboard, trying to explain the difference
between propaganda and advertising.
sometimes it wishes on a star. sometimes
it pretends to be a tugboat on the
Mississippi in 1859. sometimes it's
a relief. sometimes it surfaces
in London, claiming it never knew
the gun was loaded. sometimes it
whirls like a ballet
dancer in the middle of
a completely empty Times
Square. sometimes it simply
is not there, regardless of what
blind faith may say. sometimes
it counts all the hairs on your
head, then splits them. sometimes
it can be caught adjusting the
color control on the telescope at
the Griffith Observatory.
sometimes it peters out before you do.
sometimes it gets solar activity
to disrupt TV transmissions. sometimes
it resembles a dove flying above.
sometimes it shoots out streetlights.
sometimes it never, never stands
in a certain place overlooking

the Hudson River. sometimes it
has no remorse. sometimes it shines!
sometimes it rolls around in history.
sometimes it's as lonely as a
grave. sometimes it skydives in
the Grand Canyon. sometimes it
can be heard giving a testimony on true
love at the Taj Mahal. sometimes it takes
pictures of fat men eating. sometimes
it fastens itself on the
back of poor judgment. sometimes it holds to
truths that are self-evident. sometimes it wanders
around in the wilderness for 40 years, missing
the way out repeatedly. sometimes it's out of
focus. sometimes it has no reason
for being. sometimes it foams at the
mouth, then spits up into oblivion. sometimes
it hammers invisible nails into
smog. sometimes it simply is! sometimes it
sets a course for Easter Island. sometimes
it walks the floors at Graceland. sometimes
it has a way of fooling the wisest of men.
sometimes it leaks information to
expired newspapers. sometimes it
has no way of coping. sometimes it
circles the covered wagons   sometimes it knows no
limits. sometimes it climbs mountains
dressed in a tuxedo. sometimes it
is released from bondage. sometimes it is
functional for a few minutes.
sometimes it divides nations.
sometimes it
shimmers on the moonlit water. sometimes it runs a
race with stolen shoes. sometimes it pauses
for applause. sometimes it deals cards
from the bottom of the deck. sometimes it alters
events for diabolical purposes. sometimes it is
your friend. sometimes it jumps like a
jackrabbit into the red moon. sometimes it moves
around the bases like a 90-year-old Babe Ruth.

A Prayer for Bosses and Warmongers

DOUG DRAINE

When they are holding
the razorblades to
their *own* wrists, or cancer
is eating them away
like a ravenous
beast, crushing

their bones for
the marrow—
and no amount of
money or lies or
power
can save them

from the blades
in their own hands or
the beast of cancer
finally reducing them to ash—
I pray they remember,
seconds before they die,

all the people they have
destroyed
and oppressed and
condemned.
And I pray that *that* thought
is their last one.

Waiting Tables in Reno

DOUG DRAIME

40 years ago,
she left him
while he was
getting his
leg blown off
in 'Nam.

Now,
here she was,
waiting tables
in Reno—not even
recognizing him—
after she almost
fell over his
prosthetic leg.

"Keep your legs
under the table, *sir*.
I could've fallen and
broken something."

The Ripperology Trail

DAVID S. POINTER

The detective
used a Victorian skirt-lifter
like tweezers
          peeling back
curtain vapor

skin-flap scrapbooks in time,
information typed in reports

inside cold-case file cabinets
sutured to shadow and blood.

Our Place

NEIL SERVEN

Children lived here. Matchbox cars keep turning up in the backyard, dirt clumped in their wheel wells. Puzzle pieces behind the radiator.

Height marks penciled on the doorjamb. Finger smudges.

In the basement: a ring of woodpecker holes. Dart scores in chalk.

After papers were passed, they made the mistake of looking up the address and found the police logs. Harassment calls, officer to investigate. Neighbors hear arguing in the street. Nobody paid the broadband bill, and now the kids can't do their homework.

The husband was a landscaper, and not a bright one: whatever soil filler he used is suffocating the giant oak. Branches dying off, clattering off the gutters.

The middle child was a sleepwalker, the neighbor said. Hence, they guessed, the latch bolted to the outside of the bedroom door. Baffling: four in the morning, the doorknob rattles. Kid has to scream to pee.

Removing all of the child locks was a project.

Before the family, they were told, there was a man who lived alone for thirty years. His name is still etched on the door knocker. Never used two of the same screw to hang anything.

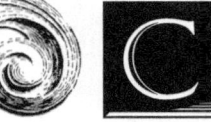

Three a.m.: Child in her nightie on the porch roof. Services rendered.

That first winter, snow didn't fall until January and then never stopped until April. They both came down with awful coughs and slept in separate rooms so as not to wake each other. But the rooms were cold and their knees biting from shoveling, and the dog would bounce back and forth between the beds, unsure whom to settle with.

There was a divorce. They were desperate to move on, and the agent—sweet lady, bony hands, master of extortion—leveraged the price down to a song.

credo

I am all for thisness
Haecceitas after Scotus
like Beckett against
monstrous nonsense

ROBERT SCHULER

Cake

This is the delicious part.
This is where I'm so anxious to please,
so serious with thrum,
so dumb with intent,
I camp out in the middle of your cocina
and stumble in the dark
for the magical ingredients
that will keep me hot and heavy
deep inside your corazón.
You mock my sticky sweet.
"We aren't sixteen," you remind me.
Oh, I know there won't be any corsages
or furtive fumbles beneath the bleachers.
You cannot pop my cherry.
You will not pop The Question.
I'm dirty and battered from the long road
that brought me to this tricky intersection.
A woman can die walking to the bakery,
her mind on galletas and black coffee,
not on the trucks zooming by.
I'll be sick of the whole thing soon enough.
I'll walk away licking frosting from my fingers.
You will look away like none of this happened.
Let's pretend like that day will never come.
This is the delicious donut, this morsel of time
that is called NOW.
I'll share every crumb with you.
This is the most delicious part,
both of us hungry for something fresh,
knowing the hell of stale
lurks with a smirk
around that tacky corner.

MISTI RAINWATER-LITES

To Kill Them to Break Them

ROBERT JAMES RUSSELL

And then came the moment in which he would have to heft the heavy felling axe and split his father's skull.

"Do it, boy," the man said, soot-mouthed from the cot in the corner. "Let's see what you're made of."

The boy crossed the single-roomed cabin to the axe hanging on the wall and lifted it from the metal hooks, could feel the smooth hickory in his hand like a jolt. As if meant for his young grip.

With weapon in hand, he looked back at the man who had sired him—lumped over and bent, dirty and broken—then surveyed the rest of the small room: Fireplace just crackling embers now, emitting that long shadow-making glow. Muddy bootprints leading in from the cold. Knife—serrated variety—lying sticky with red on the floor. Mother slumped dead in a pool of her own filth at the writing hutch with an elegance not strictly reserved for the living, skin pale like the snow falling outside.

When the boy had come upon his mother, he had been struck by the scene, studied her—her form, her arched neck, desktop stained deep red, pen still clutched in her small hand. He had tried to read the letter resting under her dead weight, but it was soaked with her fluids, and the writing had become smudged. It was then, investigating what she could've been scrawling, that he saw the smiling gash cut jaggedly across her throat and, startled, backed away.

The man had surprised the boy—moved in up behind fast from the darkest corner of the cabin—but the boy, quick and sure-footed, dodged and grabbed the knife that had been dropped—the one used for snuffing out his mother's light—and stuck the man in the gut. The boy kept hold of the handle as the man yipped, reached out with old, bone-thin fingers, scraping at the boy's face. But the boy kept steadfast, shoved the knife in deep, wiggled it in both directions, opened the man up good, and watched as blood poured ceaseless.

The man kicked the boy down and, with knife still firmly implanted, hobbled to the cot where he bled, not quiet, but loud and beastly—the way he had lived his life.

The boy had been warned by Miss DuPont—a friend of his mother's, who read futures in old chicken bones shaken up and let loose from a Van Camp's tin—that such a feat of manhood might well be in his future.

"Terrible things are waiting for you," she told him. "Be ready."

But he wasn't. Couldn't be—no way to predict such a thing. And he hated that he was out while it happened. That he wasn't here to watch over her frail being.

"C'mon! What're you waiting for!" his father howled, clutching his own gut. "Do it now!"

The boy inched closer, weight of the axe tiring his arms. Shock had worn off, and he had become cognizant of his actions, present and future; he could feel the sickness ball up in him that he had been told often accompanied the First Time. Yet, his thoughts remained on his mother: vengeance was what she deserved. So, he met the man's gaze with a matched frenzy and stood at the end of the cot.

Still kneeling, the man struggled upright and, through thick-scraggled beard, the boy could see his father's poisonous lips curl into a smile. The man was broad-shouldered and hook-nosed, like the boy, and had lived a hard life—his skin was scarred and muted and nicked from head to toe, beaten down by his travels. A life of no good.

"That's right," the man said, still smiling. "If I done one thing right in this life, it's teach you to finish what you start." He pulled out the knife, hissed and whistled through the pain, and dropped the glistening thing beside him. Laid his hands palms-up on his knees, showing he was no longer a threat. "Means anything," he said, "she had it coming."

"No," the boy said.

The man laughed "You don't know half of it. She had an evil in her needed to be snuffed out."

The boy gripped the hickory harder. "Stop."

"It's true. She done some terrible things. And me? Some bad, sure, but nothing like her actions." The man licked his lips. "You know your scriptures, boy?"

The boy thought. "Some."

"I was a farmhand down in Bristol when Raphael visited me in a dream. Flaming sword and shield. Told me it had to be this way. You ask me? I never pay no attention to you lot. Was better for it. Prob'ly you, too. But the things he showed me—visions, boy!—they wormed deep inside and couldn't let go. I had to do what he asked, you see? She an evil woman."

"No. She was good."

"You only see what she want you to. You should know that. Mind you, I'm not asking to be spared, just letting you know why I done what I done. Why this outcome has befallen you. Why I failed."

"Failed?"

"Was meant to come after you next," the man said, showing his open mouth, crowded gray teeth perched like an animal's. "That you were—"

But it had been enough, and the boy two-handed the axe back behind his own head and brought it forward again, landing it with a wet thunk in the man's skull—deep. It didn't kill the man right away: his eyes rolled up and back, side to side, his tongue wagged free from his mouth before blood followed, let loose from within, and his body convulsed, seemed almost to want to stand straight up, before it fell to the ground in a messed puddle.

The boy stood there for a bit, studied what had become of his father, replayed the man's words in his head, then looked back over at his mother again in the chair at the hutch, writing Lord-knows-what with her fancy pen. Wearing her white nightgown, black hair falling long over her back. He removed her from her seat and dragged her across the room, lumped her next to his father on the cot. Positioned them in a way as if they had been sleeping. He removed the axe, placed it back on the wall, and sat cross-legged on the floor in the center of the room, watching them, wind howling fierce outside, wondering if this was what Miss DuPont had meant.

If any of the sickness was in him, too.

If there had been another way.

33

JUSTIN HYDE

clock
officially shows
i'm old as jesus
when they
cut him down.

a few texts
dribble in
from old girlfriends

my sister

the ex-wife.

i knew
steinbeck was good

but here
he effortlessly
scoops out
the inner lives of people
like ice cream.

my phone rings.

i turn it off.

i hate birthdays

nor do i feel
any kinship
with jesus

and probably
i'll never
write anything
half as good
as this
slim novel by steinbeck.

but strangely

i'm steeled
to the task.

Plan B

I.

    The condom broke.
    The condom broke.
The condom broke.

& now we're sitting on the side
of your bed, naked in discussion.
The first serious talk we've had,
& I'm staring at the cheap plastic piece
I would tear apart with my teeth if I thought
it could feel anything like pain.

Your hair sticks up at strange angles
while you say you don't ever want kids,
say you'll pay whatever it costs to make sure,
get the pills for me even if I don't want to go.

I tell you I'll take care of it
& gather my clothes in the dark,
delete you from my phone
as I walk down the stairs,
not feeling pregnant at all.

II.

    I take a long, hot shower &
flush my vagina twice.
I don't feel pregnant at all, yet
I can't sleep, can't calm down, &
the health center won't be open for 8 hours.
I bite my nails & look up every article
written about emergency contraception.
I read statistics, side effects, affects of kidney disease,
probability of urinary-tract infections, abortion practices,
healthcare providers, reproductive rights, & legal statutes.

Now, I'm pregnant.
Really truly pregnant.
I can feel your baby
moving in my uterus,
& I want to scream.

I make strong coffee, & I bet you're asleep, all snores &
dreams, as I read about RU-486, Plan B, Ella, Orval, Preven,
IUDs, estrogen, levonorgestrel, Vitamin C, massage
techniques, the days of bloody knives & folding tables, strategic
stair falls, poisonous tinctures, back-alley doors, long hatpins,
knitting needles, & wire hangers.
My mind goes to dark places as the sun finally starts to show.

III.

I sit in my car
at the grocery store
with the pharmacy
earliest to open
that carries the pills
I've decided I need.
The coffee has left me
jittery & tasting bitter
grounds on my tongue,
& the doors are opening,
& I am rushing forward,
black jacket buttoned
against the wind.

Two pharmacists sit behind the glass
moving prescriptions from right to left,
gathering bottles & labels & laughing
while I wait. Their phone starts to ring;
people line up behind me. I grow warm
waiting for the window to slide from
left to right, waiting to spend money
I need for food next week to buy two
tiny overpriced pills, waiting ...

She smiles & slides the glass open,
motions me to approach the counter.
My request brings audible disapproval
from the Catholic grandmother directly
behind me in line. When I turn around,
not amused, she grabs the gold cross
around her neck & whispers, "Dios mio."
I give her the finger & turn back to the
window, waiting.

IV.

I am sore all over,
my body rejecting
the story of your sperm
meeting my egg
with wave upon wave
of nauseating hormones.
My skin feels electric, &
all clothes, all touch end
in pain. I cry & laugh at
the same time, my emotions
unable to fit on any chart. It
hurts to lie down; it hurts to
sit. I have no energy to stand
& crawl to the bathroom when
I must. I stay in one spot for as
long as I can, reading, watching,
staring straight ahead. I cannot
imagine what pain an abortion
attempt with a hatpin would have
brought; I don't want to at all.
These damn pills are hard enough.

I cannot sleep. I cannot eat.
I drink a full gallon of water
& curse myself, curse you,
with each sip. I want to clean
everything, to shower all day
tomorrow, to drown my room
in water & soap bubbles. I want
to float on a sea of foam & warm
water until there is nothing left
of what I once was, until last night
is erased completely. I want to wash
away to an island where no one
will ask about you ever again
& where mi coño never needs
a plan B.

One night, when the breath of August blew hotter

LEAH ANGSTMAN

"I t isn't as if you liked him. I hardly think you can feel sorry that he's lying six feet under."

"He's not exactly six feet under," Richard replied to the haughty woman as he tugged on her husband's limp arms and battled to keep the overcoat sleeves from slipping free. The battle lost, the dead man's arms dropped from the sleeves, and a pocketwatch dropped simultaneously from the pocket, slamming against Richard's polished wingtip, splattering mud droplets up his spats. Its *tick-tock-tick-tock* amplified in the darkness, the sound thudding against Richard's chest like Elda's heartbeats.

Elda. What a dame. Any man would die for her, and one did. *What a dame; what a shame*, Richard had always said. Yet, here he was, lifting Elda's fourth husband into an early grave without the bravery of questions.

He watched her clench the shovel like she would a man's heart, twisting its handle, jabbing it into the ground with repeated blows. His heart hurt from the careless repetitions, hurt like a heart would hurt if she squeezed it or drove a shovel through it.

Dawn creased the horizon by the time he'd kicked the last batch of dirt and leaves over the hidden grave.

"You didn't like him," Elda whispered again.

"No." He wiped his brow. "No, I never liked the man." There again, the *tick-tock-tick-tock* rose like a degüello, and Richard eyed the timepiece resting near the toe of his shoe. "Might I have this watch?"

"For memories, Rick?" she chuckled coldly. "Old times' sake?"

"For payoff," he returned just as coldly. "Lord knows I'm not getting what was promised from you. So you oughta think real hard about keeping me quiet."

Elda raised a brow and her pretty lips curled, but void of thought, her hands clenched tighter on the shovel.

The Courage to Breathe

HARRY CALHOUN

Since she's been gone, it feels as if you have to ask
permission to lift the Venetian blinds in the living room,
the bedroom. You must need a dispensation
for that most valuable sleep, which hangs mostly
out of your reach. "To do" sometimes becomes
the hardest verb to conjugate, staring at the list
the easiest task.

It's overcast outside, of course, dousing
the huge sunroom windows with gloom.
What speaks defiantly in this room, now,
and gives you the courage to keep breathing,
are the wedding band still proud on your finger,
two Labrador puppies faithful at your feet,
and this slow, deliberate scrawl of the first poem

since she left, the poem in longhand on your pad,
biting hard and true into the paper.

Influences of Light

It happens each early summer.
She backs off her anti-depressants,
thinking more UV rays can substitute
for her drugs. She comes out swinging,
determined to reclaim what is
rightfully hers.

For a day or a week, she's a warrior
but quickly fades into a humble,
tumble, pile of bewilderment. (It's
hard to sustain determination on
just sunlight. Warmth alone isn't
enough to help you think straight.)

Following her short freedom flight,
she becomes earthbound, a cloud
that hovers low against a county trunk
road—a vaporous curtain that flattens
and abducts you.

But you drive on, and eventually pass
through it, through her. And bring her to
a small hill where you ask her to
look a great distance
and remember tomorrow
or yesterday
or her true nature
with the ease of her
winter-fresh mind.

CHARLES P. RIES

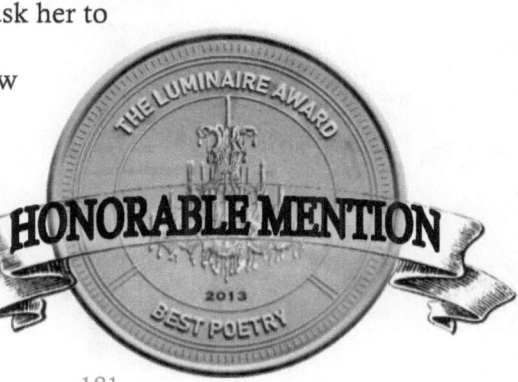

Author

[COVER ARTIST:]

Terry Fan

[Ontario, Toronto, Canada] is an illustrator who studied at Ontario College of Art & Design University and went through their interdisciplinary program. He works with ink, graphite, and Adobe Photoshop and is currently involved in a number of creative pursuits, including T-shirt design, screenwriting, graphic novels, and children's book illustration. His motto is short but poignant: "Art is my drug of choice." [society6.com/artist/igo2cairo] [Front cover artwork: "Deep Sea Garden"] [Back cover artwork: "Lost at Sea"]

Leah Angstman

[Palo Alto, California] is a transplanted Midwesterner, unsure what feels like home anymore. She writes historical fiction, poetry, and plays; has had 20 chapbooks published; and has earned two Pushcart Prize nominations. Recently, she won the 2013 Nantucket Directory Poetry Contest and took Honorable Mentions in both the 2013 *Shenandoah* Bevel Summers Prize for Short Fiction (Washington and Lee University) and the 2013 Baltimore Science Fiction Society Poetry Contest. Her work has appeared in numerous journals, including *Zygote in My Coffee*, *The Journal of Compressed Creative Arts*, *Suisun Valley Review*, and *Shenandoah*. [leahangstman.com] [pages 16, 82, 138, 178]

Luis Cuauhtémoc Berriozábal

[West Covina, California] works in the mental health field in Los Angeles. He was born in Cuernavaca, Morelos, Mexico. His first book of poems, *Raw Materials*, was published by Pygmy Forest Press, and Kendra Steiner Editions will publish his next chapbook. His poetry has appeared in English and Spanish in many print and online journals. [is.gd/madswirlLCB] [pages 49, 135]

Sean Brendan-Brown

[Olympia, Washington] is a graduate of the Iowa Writers' Workshop. A medically retired Marine, he is the author of three poetry chapbooks (*No Stopping Anytime*; *King of Wounds*; *West Is a Golden Paradise*), a fiction chapbook, *Monarch of Hatred*, and a short-story collection, *Brother Dionysus* (MilSpeak Books). He has been published in *Notre Dame Review*, *Wisconsin Review*, *Indiana Review*, *Texas Review*, *Southampton Review*, and in the University of Iowa Press anthologies: *American Diaspora* and *Like Thunder*. He is the recipient of a 1997 NEA Poetry Fellowship and a 2010 NEA Fiction Fellowship. [is.gd/facebookSBB] [Featured Writer pages 94-104]

Harry Calhoun

[Raleigh, North Carolina] has so far survived three broken ribs and three marriages, the latest by far the best and still active. He has endured countless jobs, written a ton of articles and other works, and had a few dozen books and chapbooks of poetry published. His books and chapbooks  include *I knew Bukowski like you knew a rare leaf*; *The Black Dog and the Road*; *Something Real*; *Near daybreak, with a nod to Frost*; *Retreating Aggressively into the Dark*; *The Insomnia Poems*; *Maintenance and Death*; *Retro*; *How Love Conquers the World*; and *Failure Is Unimportant*. His career has included Pushcart Prize nominations, a Sundress Best of the Net nomination, and publications in *Lily*, *Abbey*, *Orange Room Review*, *Gutter Eloquence*, *Faircloth Review*, *Thunder Sandwich*, and others. Harry lives in Raleigh, with his wife, Trina, and his dogs, Hamlet and Harriet. [harrycalhoun.net] [pages 48, 113, 180]

Paula Cary

[Green Cove Springs, Florida] is a poet, living with a wannabe pirate. Her chapbooks include *Agapornis Swinderniana* (Dancing Girl Press, 2012) and *Sister, Blood and Bone* (Blood Pudding Press, 2013). She reviews other writers at her blog, *Poet Hound*, and she hopes to spread the love of poetry through her work online and through her sidewalk-chalk art on her driveway. [poethound.blogspot.com] [page 47]

Alan Catlin

[Schenectady, New York] has been writing and publishing since the 70's. Among his many publications are some sixty chapbooks and full-length books of poetry and prose. His  most recent full-length book of poetry is, *Alien Nation*. He is the poetry editor of *Misfit Magazine*. [misfitmagazine.net] [pages 71, 114, 136]

CEE

[Normal, Illinois] is a failed short-story writer, failed novelist, and failed playwright. In the early 2000's, he developed Carpal Tunnel Syndrome, forcing him, by 2007, to fall back to the shorthand of poetry. Over 600 of his poems have since seen or will see some form of media. He has been printed in such diverse publications as *bear creek haiku*, *Jerry Jazz Musician*, *Children, Churches and Daddies*, *Tales of the Talisman*, *The Storyteller*, *Barbaric Yawp*, *The Iconoclast*, and *Dreams and Nightmares*. His poem, "It's an Old Story," received a Pushcart Prize nomination in 2009. CEE is the author of 17 chapbooks, including *12 times 12 equals Gross*, *Und ihr Habt Doch Gesiegt (You Have Finally Won)*, *I Am Not Sydney Carton*, *tomB Baby (with Hot Robert Todd)*, *Gunther*, and eight books with Alternating Current Press; and he has been included in the international mailers of Marymark Press. [pages 66, 112, 129, 141]

Christina Elaine Collins

[Burke, Virginia] is a Pushcart Prize-nominated fiction writer and an MFA candidate and teaching fellow at George Mason University. She is also the assistant editor for *So to Speak: A Feminist Journal of Language and Art* and has been a writer-in-residence at both the Kimmel Harding Nelson Center for the Arts and the Art Commune Artist-in-Residence Program in Armenia. Her fiction can be found in literary publications such as *Jabberwock Review*, *Empirical Magazine*, *Weave Magazine*, *Rose Red Review*, *Otis Nebula*, *Status Hat*, and *Cliterature Journal*. [t: @CElaineCollins] [page 56]

K. M. Dersley

[Framlingham, Suffolk, England] has had poems and articles published in *Poetry Review*, *London Magazine*, *The Rialto*, *Zygote in My Coffee*, *Thunder Sandwich*, *Laura Hird*, *Word Riot*, and others. He has performed his work in London, Cambridge, Colchester, Chelmsford, and at the Wessex Festival and the Dulwich Festival. His books include *Sketches by Derz*, *Between the Alleyways at the World's Fair*, and *Management Gold Not Me*. [f:/km.dersley] [pages 50, 144]

Doug Draime

[Medford, Oregon] emerged as a poet, short-story writer, and playwright in the literary 'underground' in Los Angeles in the late 1960's. His latest book is *More than the Alley*, a full-length poetry collection from Interior Noise Press. Also available are three chapbooks: *Los Angeles Terminal: Poems 1971-1980* (Covert Press), *Rock 'n' Roll Jizz* (Alternating Current), and an online chap, *Speed of Light* (Right Hand Pointing). Draime was awarded PEN grants in 1987, 1991, and 1992; and during the last few years, he has been nominated for several Pushcart Prizes. [is.gd/linkedinDraime] [Featured Writer pages 148-162]

Aleathia Drehmer

[Painted Post, New York] is the editor of the flash-fiction website, *In Between Altered States*, and the art editor for the online journal, *Regardless of Authority*. In a previous life, she produced a print zine called *Durable Goods* and edited for Full of Crow Press and *Zygote in My Coffee*. Her work has been published extensively in the small press, both online and in print. Her most recent poetry collection, *You Find Me Everywhere*, is available from Alternating Current. Aleathia's future is pointed toward the deep country where she hopes to see the world for what it is and put it down in words. [aleathiadrehmer.wordpress.com] [pages 69, 86, 146]

Michael Estabrook

[Acton, Massachusetts] is finally free, after 40 years of working for "The Man" and sometimes "The Woman." No more useless meetings under fluorescent lights in stuffy, windowless rooms. He can concentrate instead on making better poems and on pursuing his other interests, including: history, art, music, theater, opera, and his wife, who is still the most beautiful woman he has ever known. [f:/michael.estabrook.908] [pages 21, 91, 139]

Jason Fisk

[Elk Grove Village, Illinois] is a husband, a father of two, and a teacher, living in the suburbs of Chicago. He is the author of a collection of short stories, *Hank and Jules*; a collection of micro-fiction published by Chicago Center for Literature and Photography, *Salt Creek Anthology* a collection of poetry published by Six Gallery Press, *the fierce crackle of fragile wings*; and two poetry chapbooks published by Alternating Current, *The Sagging: Spirits & Skin* and *Decay*. [jasonfisk.com] [pages 68, 85, 134]

Lawrence Gladeview

[Denver, Colorado] is a barroom raconteur and the author of two poetry collections. His writing has been published in magazines around the world, and his books are stocked on the shelves of independent bookstores and university libraries. Lawrence lives and writes in Colorado with his wife, Rebecca. [lawrencegladeview.com] [pages 54, 90, 120]

Nathan Graziano

[Manchester, New Hampshire] is a high school teacher with an MFA in fiction writing from The University of New Hampshire. He is the author of three collections of poetry, *Not So Profound* (Green Bean Press, 2003), *Teaching Metaphors* (Sunnyoutside, 2007), and *After the Honeymoon* (Sunnyoutside, 2009); two collections of short prose, *Frostbite* (GBP, 2002) and *Hangover Breakfasts* (Bottle of Smoke Press, 2012); and several chapbooks of fiction and poetry. His work has appeared in numerous literary publications and websites such as *Word Riot*, *The Hawaii Review*, *The Good Men Project*, *Night Train*, *Rattle*, and *Nerve Cowboy*. His short story, "Fishbone," was a finalist for The Norman Mailer Award in 2011, and he has a trophy to prove it. In his spare time, he enjoys writing bios about himself in third person that make it seem like any of this crap matters. [nathangraziano.com] [Featured Writer pages 22-45]

George Held

[New York City, New York] is a seven-time Pushcart Prize nominee, a three-year Fulbright lecturer in Czechoslovakia, and a teacher of English at Queens College for 37 years. His poems, short stories, book reviews, and translations have appeared in such places as *Circumference*, *Commonweal*, *Confrontation*, and *Notre Dame Review*, and on Garrison Keillor's *The Writer's Almanac*, as well as in over two dozen anthologies. Held's 17 poetry collections include *Beyond Renewal*, *After Shakespeare: Selected Sonnets*, and *Neighbors, Books 1 and 2*: animal poems for children, illustrated by Joung Un Kim. George lives in Greenwich Village, with his wife, Cheryl. [georgeheld.blogspot.com] [page 119]

Kevin M. Hibshman

[Lancaster, Pennsylvania] was born in Philadelphia on the now-defunct Naval Base; his father was serving as a medic there. The family moved two years later to Lititz, Pennsylvania, where he spent the remainder of his childhood. Life in a sequestered village was alienating, and Kevin sought refuge in music and poetry. His first influences included rock poets, Lou Reed, Jim Morrison, and Patti Smith. Later, he fell under the spell of the Beats and began to take writing seriously. Kevin performed in a few rock bands and music projects during the late 80's/early 90's. He has edited his own poetry magazine, *Fearless*, for nearly twenty years, as it transformed from print zine to eZine. Over the past two decades, Kevin has released many chapbooks and broadsides, and his poems, reviews, and collages have been published in numerous magazines worldwide. His most recent chapbook, *Incessant Shining*, was published by Alternating Current in 2011. Kevin resides in Pennsylvania with his artist partner, William, and his cat, Siouxsie. [f:/kevin.hibshman] [page 70]

Justin Hyde

[Des Moines, Iowa] works in a women's halfway house. [pages 19, 87, 172]

Merilyn Jackson

[Philadelphia, Pennsylvania] attended Temple University, got married, had two kids, divorced, remarried, owned two cheese/gourmet food shops, divorced, married the love of her life, and since 1996, has been the *Philadelphia Inquirer's* principal dance critic. She writes for many publications on dance, theater, and literature, especially Eastern European fiction, politics, and poetry—altogether more than 800 published works because she's never stopped writing. The Pennsylvania Council on the Arts awarded her food-driven novel-in-progress, *O Solitary Host*, a Literature Fellowship. A chapter of the novel appeared in the *Massachusetts Review* in the 'Food Matters' fall 2004 issue. In 2005, she received an NEA Critics' Fellowship to Duke University. Her poetry has been published, most recently, in *Exquisite Corpse, The Rusty Nail*, and *Broad Street Review*. In 2012, she attended poetry workshops at Colgate University and Sarah Lawrence College, working with poets Peter Balakian and Tom Lux, respectively. [primeglib.com] [pages 72, 116, 133]

Angie Turner Jeffreys

[Greensboro, North Carolina] has been writing poetry since the age of six. She studied English Literature and Creative Writing at Hollins University. She also studied linguistics at University College Cork, Cork, Ireland, for one lucky semester. Angie now cares for her father's health full time.

Since college, she has worked for Open Hand Publishing, LLC, tended the flocks at a public school after-school care program, privately nannied for a couple years, and chosen to spend most of her spare time gardening and hanging with her dog. Strangely, this timeline lends itself to lots of the good, bad, sometimes the ugly, too, in writing. Enjoy. [suburbanscrawlr.com] [pages 84, 118]

Patrick Kindig

[Lansing, Michigan] recently graduated from Michigan State University, where he studied German and English with a concentration in creative writing. His poetry and fiction have been published in or are forthcoming in *Prairie Margins, The Offbeat*, and *The Red Cedar Review*. [pages 14, 73, 147]

Angela Consolo Markiewicz

[Los Angeles, California] has published four chapbooks, the most recent are *An Eye*, published by Pecan Grove Press, and *As If*, Published by Little Red Books–Lummox. Angela's publications include: *Poets/Artists*, *Full of Crow*, *Long Poem Magazine* (UK), *PRESA*, *Montserrat*, *Re)Verb*, *Sketchbook*, *Seldom Nocturne*, *Istanbul Literary Review*, *Arsenic Lobster*, *Temple/Tsunami*, *Butcher Block*, *Slipstream*, *Chiron Review*, *The Hawaii Review*, *Cerberus*, *Karamu*, *Lynx Eye*, *Pemmican*, *Blind Man's Rainbow*, and *ArtWord*. Other recognitions include two Pushcart Prize nominations and 1st and Grand Prizes from *Trellis Magazine*, *JerseyWorks*, and *Amelia*. Her childrens' stories, *The Grummel Book*, have been reissued on CD by Shoofly; and *Laura Hanson*, a novella, was serialized by *ESC! Magazine*. She has also been the Contributing Editor and Regional Editor, respectively, for the small (now defunct) journals, *Mushroom Dreams* and *The New Press Quarterly*. Her chamber opera, *One Day Less*, music by D. Javelosa, was performed at the Broad 2nd Space in Santa Monica, California. [poetacmank.blogspot.com] [pages 67, 122]

Hosho McCreesh

[Albuquerque, New Mexico] is currently writing and painting in the gypsum and caliche badlands of the American Southwest. He has work appearing widely in print, audio, and online. His books are available from Bottle of Smoke Press, Mary Celeste Press, Sunnyoutside, Orange Alert Press, and Alternating Current; broadsides are available from 10pt Press; art prints are available at society6.com. [hoshomccreesh.com] [pages 20, 92]

Frankie Metro

[Albuquerque, New Mexico] is one-third of the editorial team at Kleft Jaw Press and writes music, book, and event reviews for *Unlikely Stories* Episode: IV. He has been published in numerous online and print anthologies and journals. His first poetry chapbook, *The Anarchist's Blac Book of Poetry*, was published by Crisis Chronicles Press. [kleftjaw.weebly.com] [pages 52, 130]

Shauna Osborn

[Albuquerque, New Mexico] is a Comanche/German mestiza who works as an instructor, wordsmith, and community organizer in Albuquerque. She received her Master of Fine Arts from New Mexico State University in 2005. Shauna has won various awards for her academic research, photography, and poetry. Recently, she received a National Poetry Award from the New York Public Library. [shaunamosborn.wordpress.com] [pages 12, 80, 140, 174]

David S. Pointer

[Murfreesboro, Tennessee] is an American political poet. In Spring 2012, he was asked to become an advisory panel member at Writing For Peace. This organization teaches world peace writing to young people ages 13-19. David's two

most recent political poetry books are *The Psychobilly Princess* and *Sundrenched Nanosilver*. His recent anthology publications include, *Serial Killers 2*, *Poe-It!*, and elsewhere. [f:/david.s.pointer] [pages 46, 77, 105, 163]

D. A. Pratt

[Regina, Saskatchewan, Canada] has short articles on Charles Bukowski and Henry Miller scheduled to appear in 2013, as well as a number of other poems, many of which have been composed at Earl's South, where he can sometimes be found with a pad of paper. [t: @PrattDA] [page 111]

Misti Rainwater-Lites

[San Antonio, Texas] is the author of several collections of poetry and fiction, most recently: *Bullshit Rodeo*, available from Epic Rites Press. Misti resides in San Antonio, with her muse, a ridiculously good-looking Latino who knows how to fix things. [is.gd/blogMRL] [pages 88, 167]

Charles P. Ries

[Milwaukee, Wisconsin] has had narrative poems, short stories, interviews, and poetry reviews appear in over two hundred print and electronic publications. He has received five Pushcart Prize nominations and is the author of six books of poetry. He was awarded the Wisconsin Regional Writers Association "Jade Ring" Award for humorous poetry and is the former poetry editor of *Word Riot* and *ESC!*. He is the author of the book, *The Fathers We Find*, a somewhat-fictionalized memoir of his growing up on a mink farm in Southeastern Wisconsin, and is working on a second novel, *A Life by Invitation*. His work is archived in the Charles P. Ries Collection at Marquette University. Charles is also a founding member of the Lake Shore Surf Club, the oldest freshwater surfing club on the Great Lakes. [charlespries.com] [pages 18, 106, 181]

Christopher Robbins

[Brigantine, New Jersey] grew up in the state of ecstasy. He watched a lot of *Voltron* and Buster Keaton. His favorite Stooge is Curly Joe. [t: @Chris_Robbins] [page 132]

Robert James Russell

[Ann Arbor, Michigan] is a Pushcart Prize-nominated author and the co-founding editor of the literary journal, *Midwestern Gothic*. His work has appeared in *Pithead Chapel*, *Crime Factory*, *WhiskeyPaper*, *Joyland*, *Thunderclap! Magazine*, *The Collagist*, and *Gris-Gris*, among others. His first novel, *Sea of Trees*, is available from Winter Goose Publishing. [robertjamesrussell.com] [page 168]

Janette Schafer

[McKees Rocks, Pennsylvania] is a classically trained opera singer who has performed as a soloist for opera companies, theater houses, universities, and orchestras throughout the United States and Europe. As a writer, her poems, nonfiction

articles, and stories have appeared in over 30 literary journals, magazines, and newspapers. A collection of her poetry titled, *Other Names and Places*, was published in 2004. Her play, *Mad Virginia*, on the suicide of Virginia Woolf, recently debuted in Pittsburgh, produced by OM Productions. Janette is also Founder and Artist Director of aMUSEd artist cooperative. Lastly, she sings with the most fun groups of people you could hope to meet, in two local Pittsburgh garage bands: One O'Clock Monday and The Middle Ages. She lives in McKees Rocks, Pennsylvania, with her husband and cats. [operajan.xanga.com] [page 142]

Robert Schuler

[Menomonie, Wisconsin] is an Emeritus Professor of English, retired after 45 years of teaching. He is now studying flowers, birds, the wind, history, life. And continuing to write. His most recent book of poems, *The Book of Jeweled Visions*, is available from MWPH Books. *Poiesis Review* authors and readers can get the book from the author for a special discount of $10, shipping included. Contact Alternating Current or the author for details, if interested in this special offer. Robert is now at work on several more collections of poems. [is.gd/pwRSchuler] [pages 78, 127, 166]

Neil Serven

[Greenfield, Massachusetts] lives and works as a dictionary editor in Western Massachusetts. His stories have appeared in *Washington Square*, *Beloit Fiction Journal*, *Ayris*, *Cobalt*, *Atticus Review*, and elsewhere. [neilserven.com] [page 164]

Denis Sheehan

[Boston, Massachusetts] has been the editor/publisher of *Askew Reviews* zine for about 15 years ... and counting. His junk has appeared in *Chiron Review*, *Gonzo Parenting*, *Gloom Cupboard*, *Astoria*, *Jersey Beat*, *In Between Altered States*, *AVN Magazine*, and others, aside from his mother's fridge. He is the author of *A Nobody's Nothings*, *The Longsberry Letters*, and *Track Wreckard 1-14*. Unfortunately, more books are on the way. [boneprint.com] [pages 79, 128, 137]

Jane Stuart

[Greenup, Kentucky] lives in a family home that is now in the middle of a nature preserve. Her writing interest is poetry—traditional forms (cinquain, sonnet, villanelle, haiku, tanka) and some free verse. She enjoys making bread, doing counted cross-stitch, making cross-stitch quilt tops, and observing nature. She's delighted to have a (favorite!) poem in this issue. [page 11]

William Taylor, Jr.

[San Francisco, California] currently lives and writes in the Tenderloin neighborhood of San Francisco. His books of poetry include *Words for Songs Never Written* and *The Hunger Season*. *An Age of Monsters*, his first book of fiction, is available from Epic

Rites Press, along with his latest book of poetry, *Broken When We Got Here. The Blood of a Tourist*, a collection of new poems, is forthcoming from Sunnyoutside Press. [f:/Williamtaylorjr] [pages 65, 110]

Travis Turner

[Tuscaloosa, Alabama] writes fiction and teaches literature at the University of Alabama. Son of the Blackbelt. Lover of good bourbon & better storytelling. [f:/travisturnerfanpage] [page 124]

Paula Anne Yup

[Majuro, Marshall Islands] has written poetry since her childhood in Arizona, and later at Occidental College; her MFA is from the Vermont College program. Her 100+ poems have appeared in anthologies, including, *Feather, Fins & Fur, Earth Beneath, Sky Beyond, A Kiss Is Still a Kiss, What Book!?*, and journals, including *Earth's Daughters, Off the Coast, California Quarterly*, and *Mid-American Review*. Her first book, *Making a Clean Space in the Sky*, was recently published by Evening Street Press. She has lived in the Republic of the Marshall Islands for a decade and sometimes gets homesick, even in paradise. [page 115]

The Luminaire

Alternating Current is dedicated to nurturing and promoting the independent press and its authors. We proudly honor our authors with three annual writing awards: The Luminaire Award for Best Prose, The Luminaire Award for Best Poetry, and The Charter Oak Award for Best Historical.

The Luminaire Award is awarded annually to one work of poetry and one work of prose that have been submitted to and published by Alternating Current. All works submitted to Alternating Current are considered for the award and for publication, and we welcome readers to let us know where we can find outstanding work of merit so that we may invite those authors to submit their work to us, as well.

The winning pieces receive print publication in *Poiesis Review*; online publication on our website; two complimentary copies each of the *Poiesis Review* print journal with the winning pieces indicated with our medallion imprint; certificates; $100 honorariums; and our virtual medallion with permission for use on the authors' websites and/or any published books or online outlets.

Two honorable mention winners in each category receive print publication in *Poiesis Review*; publication on our website; one complimentary copy each of the *Poiesis Review* print journal with the honorable mention pieces indicated; and certificates.

Alternating Current is pleased to present a select panel of editors, publishers, writing instructors, literary organization members, and/or published authors who are invited by our press to participate in the blind judging process to select the winning pieces each year. The winners are announced with the annual release of each issue of *Poiesis Review* on May 15th. The judging process consists of all Alternating Current editors deciding on the top pieces for the finalist round. Those pieces are then sent blindly to the external judging panel, and the top three pieces in each category are determined by those judges via a ranking system. The judges' decisions are final. For fairness, Alternating Current editors or affiliated members are not eligible to compete for the award, and Alternating Current editors do not determine the final outcome.

2013 Judges

John Berbrich is editor of the journal *Dwarf Planet*; co-editor of the journal *Barbaric Yawp*; co-publisher at BoneWorld Publishing and MuscleHead Press; and author of the books, *The Big Whole Thing*, *Mullet*, *Balancing Act*, *A History of Post-Contemporary Poetry*, and *The Shade Returneth.*

Aleathia Drehmer is editor of the online flash fiction journal *In Between Altered States*; co-editor of the online poetry and art journal *Regardless of Authority*; former editor of *Full of Crow Poetry*, *MUST*, and *Durable Goods*; former co-editor of *Outsider Writers* and *Zygote in My Coffee*; and author of the books, *A Quiet Learning Curve*, *You Find Me Everywhere*, *Circles*, and *Thickets of Mayapple.*

J. Lewis Fleming is former editor and publisher of the journals *nibble*, *Cranial Tempest*, and *CannedPhlegm*; and author of the books, *The Bones of Saints Under Glass*, *Shades of Green*, *Why Is My Lemon Tea Red*, *Beneath a Willow*, and *Delirious and Purple*.

Brian W. Fugett is editor of the journal *Zygote in My Coffee*; publisher at Tainted Coffee Press; organizer and host of poetry readings and festivals ranging geographically from Toledo, Ohio, to Oakland, California, and everywhere in between; host of the BlogTalkRadio show *Nothing to Lose*, presented by Project U Radio Network; and occasional camera operator and special-effects assistant on TV and film projects for The Disney Channel and HBO.

Michele McDannold is founder of The Literary Underground, including the successful Project U Radio Network; editor of *Citizens for Decent Literature*; co-organizer of the touring poetry festivals Zygote in My Fez and Zyfez (a collaboration of the outfits behind *Zygote in My Coffee* and *Red Fez*); former editor at Red Fez Publications, The Guild of Outsider Writers, Rural Messengers Press, and of the publications *Red Fez*, *Red Reader*, *Lit Circus*, and *Side of Grits*; former member of The Guild of Outsider Writers and APA Centauri; former judge for the Jack Micheline Memorial Poetry Contest; and author of the books, *Slow but Steady* and *Private Vacancy*.

THE LUMINAIRE AWARD

Acknowledgments

 Special acknowledgment and thanks to Devin Byrnes and SuA Kang of Hardly Square, for their creativity in designing our Luminaire Award medallion imprint. Hardly Square is a strategy-, branding-, and design-based boutique located in Baltimore, Maryland,  that specializes in graphic design, web design, and eLearning courses. Their invaluable design expertise has made our annual awards come to life. Find out more about them at hardlysquare.com.

A very special thank you goes out to our Kickstarter donors, without whom this issue simply would not exist. Thank you, especially, to these precious few literary rockstars whose donations of $100 or more fueled us into the oncoming year: Elaine Angstman, The Camel Saloon, Craig Desjardins, Daniel Harrison, Aaron Herfurth, Jeremy Laszlo, Dennis & Marta Litos, Out of Print, Charles P. Ries, Victor Schwartzman, Justin V. Smith, Debbie Soper, and Victoria Terry. Here's lookin' at you, kids.

Alternating Current wishes to acknowledge the following publications where pieces from issue No. 6 first appeared: "New Mexico farmhouse, hard to find after all those years" first appeared in a shorter version on *In Between Altered States*, Episode 33. "Redhead" and "Influences of Light" first appeared in *Free Verse* and in Charles P. Ries' Alternating Current collection, *Girl Friend & Other Mysteries of Love*. "Vandals" first appeared in this version on Alternating Current on *Go Read Your Lunch*, with an earlier version first published in *Sententia*. "Opening Day" and "The Androgynous Coat" first appeared on *Fried Chicken and Coffee*. "Beans" first appeared in *Fiction 365*. "Girlhood Games" first appeared in Paula Cary's Blood Pudding Press chapbook, *Sister, Blood and Bone*. "The Efficacy of Poetry" first appeared in *Broad Street*

Review. "My Sister's Miscarriage" first appeared in *The Orange Room Review* and in Jason Fisk's Alternating Current chapbook, *The Sagging: Spirits & Skin*. "Choice" first appeared on *SubtleTea*. "Near to Him" first appeared on Alternating Current on *Go Read Your Lunch* and in Charles P. Ries' collection, *The Fathers We Find*. "She was one of those" first appeared in *nibble*. "Polska" and "Dormant" first appeared in *Exquisite Corpse*. "Caring" first appeared in *Eunoia Review*. "D. H. Lawrence and *The Man Who Died*" first appeared in *ZYX* No. 63. "Not every bird can be a songbird" first appeared on *Cyclamens and Swords: Birds Edition*. "Estimated Losses" first appeared in Aleathia Drehmer's Alternating Current chapbook, *You Find Me Everywhere*. "Vortex Crossing" first appeared in *Concrete Meat Sheet*. "When I Was Preparing for War" first appeared in *Problem Child Magazine*. "Carnival Poem" first appeared in *Chickasaw Plum*. "On Elvis Presley's Birthday" first appeared in *Dead King of Memphis* and on Alternating Current in Doug Draime's chapbook, *Rock 'n' Roll Jizz*. "Near the Borderline" first appeared in *Underground Voices*. "Name-Dropping for a Deceased Wife" first appeared in *Los Angeles Review*, *L.A. Weekly*, and *Gloom Cupboard*. "Sometimes" first appeared in *Paris Bitter Heartspit*. "A Prayer for Bosses and Warmongers" first appeared in *The American Dissident* and *Central Ave*. "Waiting Tables in Reno" first appeared in *Rusty Truck* and *Barbaric Yawp*. "Vortex Crossing," "Carnival Poem," "On Elvis Presley's Birthday," "Near the Borderline," "Sometimes," and "Waiting Tables in Reno" also appeared in Doug Draime's Interior Noise Press collection, *More than the Alley*. "Our Place" first appeared in *Durable Goods* No. 80. "One night, when the breath of August blew hotter" first appeared on *In Between Altered States*, Episode 34. "The Courage to Breathe" first appeared in *The Faircloth Review*.

Colophon

The edition you are holding is the First Edition pressing of this publication.

Our *Poiesis Review* logo is set in The King & Queen Font, created by bran, and in Mary Jane Larabie, created by Apostrophic Labs. The 6 and non-standard text of the title pages, all interior title fonts, the biography name headers, and The Luminaire Award judges headers, are set in Mary Jane Larabie. The drop capitals are set in Imperator Plaque, created by Paul Lloyd. All other fonts are set in Calisto MT. All fonts are used with permission; all rights reserved.

The octopus on the title page, the vintage scroll cornerpieces throughout the book, the Spencerian banner prose section divider, the vintage banner of the honorable mention awards, and the luminaire chandelier graphic are in the public domain, courtesy of The Graphics Fairy. The Alternating Current lightbulb logo was created by Leah Angstman, © 2013 Alternating Current Arts Co-op. The Luminaire Award medallion imprints were created by SuA Kang and Devin Byrnes of Hardly Square, for Alternating Current's sole use. The QR codes were created with the QR Droid generator (To read QR codes on your smartphone, we recommend downloading QR Droid for Android or Zapper Scanner for iPhone.). The Hardly Square logo is © Hardly Square, hardlysquare.com. All graphics are used with permission; all rights reserved.

The editors wish to thank the font and graphic creators for allowing legal use.

alternatingcurrentarts.com